Common Core Connections
Math
Grade 5

Carson-Dellosa Publishing, LLC
Greensboro, North Carolina

MAY 15

Credits
Content Editor: Heather Stephan
Copy Editor: Karen Seberg

 Visit *carsondellosa.com* for correlations to Common Core, state, national, and Canadian provincial standards.

Carson-Dellosa Publishing, LLC
PO Box 35665
Greensboro, NC 27425 USA
carsondellosa.com

ISBN 978-1-62442-791-6

03-293141151

Table of Contents

Introduction

What are the Common Core State Standards for Mathematics?

The standards are a shared set of expectations for each grade level in the area of mathematics. They define what students should understand and should be able to do. The standards are designed to be more rigorous and allow for students to justify their thinking. They reflect the knowledge that is necessary for success in college and beyond.

The following are Standards for Mathematical Practice as outlined in the Common Core State Standards:
1. Make sense of problems and persevere in solving them.
2. Reason abstractly and quantitatively.
3. Construct viable arguments and critique the reasoning of others.
4. Model with mathematics.
5. Use appropriate tools strategically.
6. Attend to precision.
7. Look for and make use of structure.
8. Look for and express regularity in repeated reasoning.*

How to Use This Book

The book is a collection of practice pages aligned to the Common Core State Standards for Mathematics as appropriate for fifth grade. Included is an alignment matrix so that you can see exactly which standards are addressed on each practice page. Also included are a skill assessment and skill assessment analysis. Use the test at the beginning of the year or at any time of year you wish to assess your students' mastery of certain standards. The analysis connects each test item to a practice page or set of practice pages so that you can review skills with students who struggle in certain areas.

* © Copyright 2010. National Governors Association Center for Best Practices and Chief State School Officers. All rights reserved.

Common Core State Standards*
Alignment Matrix

Pages	5.OA.1	5.OA.2	5.OA.3	5.NBT.1	5.NBT.2	5.NBT.3	5.NBT.3a	5.NBT.3b	5.NBT.4	5.NBT.5	5.NBT.6	5.NBT.7	5.NF.1	5.NF.2	5.NF.3	5.NF.4	5.NF.4a	5.NF.4b	5.NF.5	5.NF.5a	5.NF.5b	5.NF.6	5.NF.7	5.NF.7a	5.NF.7b	5.NF.7c	5.MD.1	5.MD.2	5.MD.3	5.MD.3a	5.MD.3b	5.MD.4	5.MD.5	5.MD.5a	5.MD.5b	5.MD.5c	5.G.1	5.G.2	5.G.3	5.G.4
12	●																																							
13	●																																							
14		●																																						
15		●																																						
16		●																																						
17		●																																						
18			●																																					
19			●																																					
20				●																																				
21					●																																			
22					●																																			
23						●		●																																
24						●	●																																	
25						●																																		
26						●		●																																
27									●																															
28										●																														
29											●																													
30										●	●																													
31												●																												
32												●																												
33												●																												
34												●																												
35												●																												
36												●																												
37												●																												
38												●																												
39												●																												
40												●																												
41												●																												
42													●																											
43													●																											
44													●																											
45													●																											
46													●																											
47													●																											
48													●																											
49														●																										
50														●																										
51														●																										

Common Core State Standards*
Alignment Matrix

Pages	5.OA.1	5.OA.2	5.OA.3	5.NBT.1	5.NBT.2	5.NBT.3	5.NBT.3a	5.NBT.3b	5.NBT.4	5.NBT.5	5.NBT.6	5.NBT.7	5.NF.1	5.NF.2	5.NF.3	5.NF.4	5.NF.4a	5.NF.4b	5.NF.5	5.NF.5a	5.NF.5b	5.NF.6	5.NF.7	5.NF.7a	5.NF.7b	5.NF.7c	5.MD.1	5.MD.2	5.MD.3	5.MD.3a	5.MD.3b	5.MD.4	5.MD.5	5.MD.5a	5.MD.5b	5.MD.5c	5.G.1	5.G.2	5.G.3	5.G.4
52														•																										
53															•																									
54															•																									
55																•	•																							
56																•	•																							
57																•																								
58																			•	•	•																			
59																						•																		
60																						•																		
61																						•																		
62																	•	•				•																		
63																							•	•	•															
64																							•	•	•	•														
65																							•	•	•	•	•													
66																							•	•	•	•														
67														•		•							•																	
68													•		•								•																	
69																											•													
70																											•													
71																											•													
72																											•													
73																											•													
74																											•													
75																												•												
76																													•	•	•	•								
77																														•	•	•								
78																																	•	•	•					
79																																	•	•	•					
80																																	•	•	•					
81																																	•	•	•					
82																																	•		•					
83																												•													
84																																				•				
85																																					•			
86																																					•			
87																																					•	•		
88																																							•	•
89																																							•	•
90																																							•	•

Name_____

1. Evaluate the expression. $4 + (6 - 2)$	2. Evaluate the expression. $(5 + 6) \times (2 + 4)$

3. Write a numerical expression for *6 times the sum of 3 and 7.*

4. Explain the pattern in the table.

Week	1	2	3	4	5
Savings Account	$10	$20	$30	$40	$50

5. Write the number 455 in expanded form. Describe the relationship between the two 5s.

6. Multiply 56×10^3 by moving the decimal point.

7. Write the decimal.

sixty-five hundredths

8. Write the decimal.

three and four-thousandths

9. Compare using <, >, or =.

A. 0.08 $\bigcirc$ 0.081

B. 3.934 $\bigcirc$ 3.834

10. Round each number to the nearest hundredth.

A. 3.642 _____

B. 0.372 _____

Evaluate each expression.

11.	12.
$\begin{array}{r} 342 \\ \times\ 256 \\ \hline \end{array}$	$54\overline{)7{,}452}$

13.	14.
$\begin{array}{r} 4.56 \\ +\ 2.34 \\ \hline \end{array}$	$8 - 3.45 =$

15.	16.
$\begin{array}{r} 3.56 \\ \times\ 2.3 \\ \hline \end{array}$	$7\overline{)6.37}$

17.	18.
$\begin{array}{r} 6.25 \\ +\ 3.45 \\ \hline \end{array}$	$3\frac{2}{3} + 4\frac{1}{2} =$

19.	20.
$\frac{4}{7} + 2\frac{4}{5} =$	$\frac{5}{7} - \frac{2}{3} =$

21. Elizabeth ran $\frac{2}{3}$ mile and Carter ran $\frac{1}{4}$ mile. How much farther did Elizabeth run than Carter?

22. Amanda has 10 cups of batter to make 16 cupcakes. How many cups of batter will she use for each cupcake?

23. Multiply.

$\frac{4}{9} \times \frac{2}{3} =$

24. Multiply.

$3\frac{1}{2} \times 5\frac{2}{5} =$

25. If you multiply 6 by a fraction greater than 1, is your answer greater than or less than 6?

26. There are 32 students in a PE class. Of the students, $\frac{1}{4}$ are girls. How many girls are in the class?

27. Divide.

$8 \div \frac{1}{4} =$

28. Divide.

$\frac{2}{3} \div 6 =$

29. Write the equivalent weight or measure.

6,000 grams = _____ kilograms

30. Write the equivalent weight or measure.

24 inches = _____ feet

Find the volume.

31.　　l = 5 cm, w = 2 cm, h = 3 cm	32.　　l = 3 in., w = 1 in., h = 7 in.
33.　　l = 10 m, w = 8 m, h = 2 m	34.　　l = 6 ft., w = 4 ft., h = 2 ft.

Identify the coordinates of each given point.

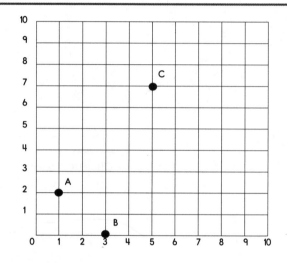

35. A (_____,_____)

36. B (_____,_____)

37. C (_____,_____)

Name the shape by its number of sides.

38. 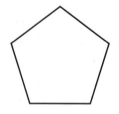 _____	39. 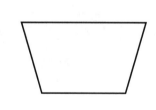 _____

40. Name the four-sided figures that have two pairs of parallel sides and four right angles.

10

After you review your student's skill assessment, match those problems answered incorrectly to the Common Core State Standards below. Pay special attention to the pages that fall into these problem sections, and ensure that your student receives supervision in these areas. In this way, your student will strengthen these skills.

Answer Key: 1. 8; 2. 66; 3. 6 × (3 + 7); 4. weeks increase by 1, account increases by $10; 5. 400 + 50 + 5, The 5 on the left is 10 times more than the 5 on the right. 6. 56,000; 7. 0.65; 8. 3.004; 9A. <; B. >; 10A. 3.64; B. 0.37; 11. 87,552; 12. 138; 13. 6.9; 14. 4.55; 15. 8.188; 16. 0.91; 17. 9.7; 18. $8\frac{1}{6}$; 19. $3\frac{13}{35}$; 20. $\frac{1}{21}$; 21. $\frac{5}{12}$ mile; 22. $\frac{5}{8}$ cup; 23. $\frac{8}{27}$; 24. $18\frac{9}{10}$; 25. greater than; 26. 8 girls; 27. 32; 28. $\frac{1}{9}$; 29. 6 kilograms; 30. 2 feet; 31. 30 cubic centimeters; 32. 21 cubic inches; 33. 160 cubic meters; 34. 48 cubic feet; 35. (1,2); 36. (3,0); 37. (5,7); 38. pentagon; 39. quadrilateral; 40. rectangle, square

Common Core State Standards*		Test Item(s)	Practice Page(s)
Operations and Algebraic Thinking			
Write and interpret numerical expressions.	5.OA.1–5.OA.2	1–3	12–17
Analyze patterns and relationships.	5.OA.2	4	18, 19
Number and Operations in Base Ten			
Understand the place value system.	5.NBT.1–5.NBT.4	5–10	20–27
Perform operations with multi-digit whole numbers and with decimals to hundredths.	5.NBT.5–5.NBT.7	11–17	28–41
Numbers and Operations—Fractions			
Use equivalent fractions as a strategy to add and subtract fractions.	5.NF.1–5.NF.2	18–21	42–52, 67, 68
Apply and extend previous understandings of multiplication and division to multiply and divide fractions.	5.NF.3–5.NF.7	22–28	53–68
Measurement and Data			
Convert like measurement units within a given measurement system.	5.MD.1	29, 30	65, 69–74, 83
Geometric measurement: understand concepts of volume and relate volume to multiplication and division.	5.MD.3–5.MD.5	31–34	76–84
Geometry			
Graph points on the coordinate plane to solve real-world and mathematical problems.	5.G.1–5.G.2	35–37	85–87
Classify two-dimensional figures into categories based on their properties.	5.G.3–5.G.4	38–40	88–90

Solve the problem within groupings first.

Example: 3 × (5 + 4)
          3 × 9 = 27

Evaluate each expression. Look for your answer swimming in the sea of answers.

1. 2 × (4 – 2)	2. (3 + 13) – (2 + 8)
3. (452 – 448) × 6	4. (18 – 3) × 6
5. 2 × [5 × (3 + 7)]	6. 500 – [3 × (20 + 80)]

☐ I can solve expressions with parentheses or brackets.

© Carson-Dellosa • CD-104606

Evaluate each expression.

1. $3 + (8 - 1)$	2. $(16 - 7) \times 5$
3. $3 \times [8 + (5 - 1)]$	4. $(7 + 3) + (12 - 7)$
5. $(3 + 5) \times (4 + 8)$	6. $11 + (13 - 8)$
7. $3 + \{20 - [3 \times (2 + 4)]\}$	8. $6 + (3 + 12) - 2$

☐ I can solve expressions with parentheses or brackets.

Add 4 and 2 and then multiply by 5.

The order of operations says to multiply first.
But the expression uses the word *then* to explain that the multiplication needs to happen *after* addition.

Use grouping symbols such as parentheses to write the expression.

$(4 + 2) \times 5$ or $5 \times (4 + 2)$

Write each sentence as a numerical expression.

1. Add 5 and 6 and then multiply by 3.

2. Subtract 7 from 15 and then multiply by 4.

3. Add 6 and 10, subtract your answer from 20, and then multiply by 2.

4. Multiply the sums of 5 and 6 and 3 and 4.

5. Multiply the sum of 4 and 6 by 7.

6. Divide the sum of 5 and 9 by 2.

☐ **I can write and interpret numerical expressions.**

Explain in words the steps for evaluating each numerical expression.

1. 5 + (3 – 1)	2. (3 + 6) × (2 – 1)
3. (6 + 12) ÷ 3	4. 4 + [10 – (4 + 2)]
5. (12 + 6) ÷ (3 + 3)	6. 8 × (16 - 8)
7. 4 + (10 + 2) – 3	8. 6 + {20 + [10 ÷ (3 + 2)]}

☐ I can interpret numerical expressions.

Explain in words the steps for evaluating each numerical expression.

1. $4 \times (7 - 1)$	2. $(3 + 7) - (2 + 1)$
3. $47 - (3 + 6)$	4. $50 \div (25 \times 2)$
5. $21 - [8 \times (5 - 3)]$	6. $5 \times (5 + 1) \div 2$
7. $(19 - 3) \div 8$	8. $[4 \times (2 + 1)] \times [(22 \div 11) + 18]$

❏ I can interpret numerical expressions.

Draw a line to match each expression with the phrase that describes it.

1. 3 times larger than the sum of 4 and 9

A. 20 − (3 + 4)

2. 20 less the sum of 3 and 4

B. (2 + 5) × (6 + 10)

3. the quotient of 15 and the sum of 2 and 3

C. (10 + 8) ÷ (10 − 7)

4. the product of the sums of 2 and 5 and 6 and 10

D. (12 − 7) × 3

5. 6 times larger than the difference of 10 and 7

E. (4 + 5) × 8

6. the quotient of the sum of 10 and 8 and the difference of 10 and 7

F. 6 × (10 − 7)

7. the sum of 4 and 5 multiplied by 8

G. 15 ÷ (2 + 3)

8. the difference of 12 and 7 multiplied by 3

H. 3 × (4 + 9)

☐ **I can write and interpret numerical expressions.**

Name_____

Use the information to complete each section of the table.

A new country artist sold 1 million copies of his first album, 3 million copies of his second album, and 5 million copies of his third album. If the pattern continues, how many copies will he sell when he makes his fifth album?

1. Explain the pattern in words.	2.

Album Number	Records Sold (in Millions)
1	
2	
3	
4	
5	

3. Use the table to make a list of ordered pairs in question 2. The first pair has been done for you.

(1,1)

4. Graph your points on the coordinate plane below.

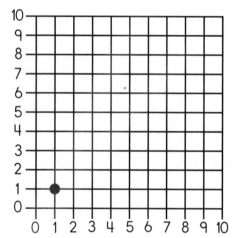

5. He will sell _____ copies of his fifth album.

☐ I can use given rules to generate numerical patterns, form ordered pairs, and graph the ordered pairs on a coordinate plane.

18

Name_____

Use the information to complete each section of the table.

Long-distance swimmers generally need to take more breaths as they near the end of a race.
On lap 2, Mark took 2 breaths; he took 3 breaths on lap 4, and he took 4 breaths on lap 6.
If the pattern continues, how many breaths will Mark take on lap 10?

1. Explain the pattern in words.	2.

Lap Number	Breaths
2	
4	
6	
8	
10	

3. Use the table to make a list of ordered pairs in question 2. The first pair has been done for you.

(2,2)

4. Graph your points on the coordinate plane below.

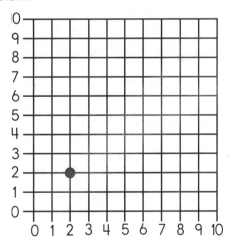

5. He will take _____ breaths on lap 10.

☐ **I can use given rules to generate numerical patterns, form ordered pairs, and graph the ordered pairs on the coordinate plane.**

How many tenths are in 34?

Use the nearest place values to find a more specific answer. Start at the decimal point. Look to the right to find tenths or hundredths. Look to the left to find ones, tens, or hundreds.

$$34.0$$

There are 40 tenths in 34.

Answer each question. Some answers may be written as decimals.

1. How many tens are in 85?

2. How many tenths are in 5?

3. How many tens are in 235?

4. How many hundredths are in 0.5?

5. How many tens are in 153?

6. How many ones are in 512.5?

7. How many tenths are in 15.03?

8. Circle two numbers above. Explain how the 5s are different.

☐ **I understand the place value of a number.**

Explain how many times you would move the decimal point and in which direction to solve each problem.

1. 5×10^2	2. 3×10^5
3. $50 \div 10^3$	4. $125 \div 10$
5. $840 \div 10^2$	6. 675×10^2
7. 10.034×10^4	8. $800.01 \div 10^4$

☐ **I understand how to move a decimal point when multiplying or dividing by a power of 10.**

To multiply by 10, move the decimal point **one** place to the right.	To multiply by 100, move the decimal point **two** places to the right.	To multiply by 1,000, move the decimal point **three** places to the right.
0.4	**0.40**	**0.400**
$10 \times 0.4 = 4$	$100 \times 0.4 = 40$	$1,000 \times 0.4 = 400$

Find each product. Use mental math.

1. $10 \times 0.06 =$ $100 \times 0.06 =$ $1,000 \times 0.06 =$ $10 \times 0.6 =$

2. $10 \times 4.3 =$ $100 \times 4.3 =$ $1,000 \times 4.3 =$ $0.43 \times 100 =$

3. $0.653 \times 1,000 =$ $1.09 \times 10 =$ $21.3 \times 10 =$ $10 \times 0.007 =$

4. $1,000 \times 0.046 =$ $0.46 \times 1,000 =$ $0.46 \times 100 =$ $0.46 \times 10 =$

5. $1,000 \times 3.9 =$ $0.0045 \times 10 =$ $100 \times 0.03 =$ $12.6 \times 1,000 =$

6. $1.234 \times 100 =$ $0.11 \times 1,000 =$ $0.11 \times 10,000 =$ $0.11 \times 100,000 =$

☐ **I can correctly place the decimal point when multiplying a decimal by a power of 10.**

Comparing decimals is similar to comparing whole numbers.
1. Line up the numbers by place value.
2. Compare the digits from left to right.

Example 1 0.08 ◯ 0.8

1. Align: 0.08
                   0.8
2. Compare. After the decimal point, you have a 0 and an 8. Because 8 is greater than 0, the greater number is 0.8.

0.08 (<) 0.8

Example 2 11.13 ◯ 11.03

1. Align: 11.13
                   11.03
2. Compare. The 11s before the decimal point are the same. After the decimal point, because 1 is greater than 0, the greater number is 1.

11.13 (>) 11.03

Compare using <, >, or =.

1. 0.007 ◯ 0.07

2. 0.08 ◯ 0.8

3. 2.159 ◯ 2.259

4. 101.05 ◯ 101.005

5. 10.05 ◯ 10.005

6. 9.50 ◯ 7.05

7. 0.99 ◯ 0.009

8. 214.01 ◯ 214.001

9. 30.249 ◯ 30.429

10. 9.008 ◯ 9.08

11. 0.004 ◯ 4.00

12. 614.05 ◯ 614.05

13. 6.041 ◯ 6.401

14. 8.26 ◯ 8.026

15. 92.001 ◯ 92.001

16. 43.014 ◯ 43.104

17. 263.08 ◯ 263.81

18. 0.83 ◯ 0.63

☐ **I can use >, =, and < to compare two decimals to the thousandths place based on values of the digits in each place.**

You should already know the place value names for numbers greater than 0. There are also names for place values after the decimal place.

thousands	hundreds	tens	ones		tenths	hundredths	thousandths
1	2	4	5	.	1	7	6

Study the following:

Decimal	Read As	Equivalent Fractions
0.1	one-tenth	$\frac{1}{10}$
0.7	seven-tenths	$\frac{7}{10}$
0.23	twenty-three hundredths	$\frac{23}{100}$
0.05	five-hundredths	$\frac{5}{100}$
0.783	seven hundred eighty-three thousandths	$\frac{783}{1000}$
0.045	forty-five thousandths	$\frac{45}{1000}$
2.6	two and six-tenths	$2\frac{6}{10}$
15.01	fifteen and one-hundredth	$5\frac{1}{100}$

Hint: Use "and" to separate a whole number from a fraction.

Fill in the blanks with the missing information.

1. 0.3   three-tenths   _____

2. 1.12   _____   _____

3. _____   two hundred twenty-one thousandths   _____

4. _____   _____ $\frac{53}{100}$

5. 0.871   _____   _____

6. _____   _____ $2\frac{1}{100}$

☐ I can read and write decimals to the thousandths place.

Name_____

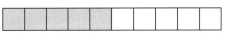

$\frac{5}{10}$ or 0.5

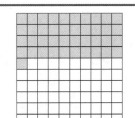

$\frac{41}{100}$ or 0.41

Write the fraction and the decimal for each figure.

	Fraction	Decimal

1. 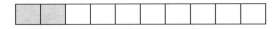 _____ _____

2. 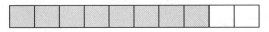 _____ _____

3. 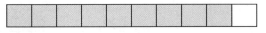 _____ _____

4. 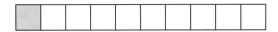 _____ _____

5. 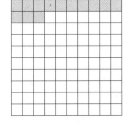 _____ _____

6. 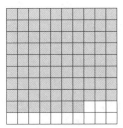 _____ _____

7. 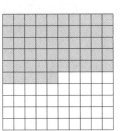 _____ _____

☐ I can use decimals to show understanding of place value.

Put the prices on the menu in order from least to greatest.

$1.25 $2.03 $1.07 $2.51 $1.10 $2.15 $2.21 $1.05

Item	Price
Bottled Water	
Milk	
Fries	
Salad	
Cheese Sandwich	
Tuna Sandwich	
Hamburger	
Cheeseburger	

Circle the greatest number in each row.

1. 4.05   4.50   4.005   4.15   4.55   4.5

2. 10.57   10.49   10.005   10.057   10.75   10.094

3. 2.5   2.15   2.52   2.005   2.095   2.51

4. 1.8   1.84   1.48   1.847   1.75   1.5

5. 89.90   88.19   8.90   89.09   89.5   89.01

☐ I can compare decimals based on digits in each place.
☐ I can use place value to compare and order decimals from least to greatest.

Round each number to the nearest tenth.

1. 0.57   2. 0.978

3. 1.56   4. 3.087

Round each number to the nearest hundredth.

5. 6.3465   6. 3.14579

7. 0.0081   8. 2.5869

Round each decimal to the nearest tenth and hundredth.

9. 3.0184   10. 29.962

☐ I can round decimals to any place.

Step 1
Multiply by the
ones digit.

$$
\begin{array}{r}
{\scriptstyle 2} \\
8\,7\,2 \\
\times\ 4\,9\,4 \\
\hline
3,4\,8\,8
\end{array}
$$

4 × 872 = 3,488

Step 2
Multiply by the
tens digit.

$$
\begin{array}{r}
{\scriptstyle 6\ 1} \\
8\,7\,2 \\
\times\ 4\,9\,4 \\
\hline
3,4\,8\,8 \\
7\,8,4\,8\,\underline{0}
\end{array}
$$

90 × 872 = 78,480

Step 3
Multiply by the
hundreds digit.

$$
\begin{array}{r}
{\scriptstyle 2} \\
8\,7\,2 \\
\times\ 4\,9\,4 \\
\hline
3,4\,8\,8 \\
7\,8,4\,8\,\underline{0} \\
3\,4\,8,8\,\underline{0\,0}
\end{array}
$$

400 × 872 = 348,800

Step 4
Add.

$$
\begin{array}{r}
8\,7\,2 \\
\times\ 4\,9\,4 \\
\hline
3,4\,8\,8 \\
7\,8,4\,8\,0 \\
+\ 3\,4\,8,8\,0\,0 \\
\hline
4\,3\,0,7\,6\,8
\end{array}
$$

Multiply.

1. 762
   ×381

2. 2,503
   × 741

3. 638
   × 897

4. 982
   × 872

5. 594
   × 439

6. 287
   × 287

7. 758
   × 439

8. 165
   × 825

9. 284
   × 833

10. 477
    × 360

11. 383
    × 103

12. 460
    × 342

13. 598
    × 636

14. 963
    × 328

15. 789
    ×951

16. 4,610
    × 239

17. 3,944
    × 307

18. 2,775
    × 173

19. 1,615
    × 239

20. 2,138
    × 256

21. 1,953
    × 279

22. 3,126
    × 382

23. 8,362
    × 123

24. 1,234
    × 228

25. 2,434
    × 327

☐ I can multiply multi-digit whole numbers.

Divide 32$\overline{)7,980}$

Step 1
There are not enough thousands to divide. Estimate to place the first digit in the quotient.

Use rounding to estimate.

Think: 30$\overline{)80}$
80 ÷ 30 is about 2

The first digit of the quotient will be in the hundreds place.

Step 2
Multiply. Subtract. Compare. Bring down the next digit.

```
        2
32 ) 7,980      Multiply 2 × 32
    -64         Subtract 79 - 64
    158         Compare 15 < 32
                Bring down the 8.
```

The digits are really coming down today!

Step 3
Multiply. Subtract. Compare. Bring down the next digit.

```
      249r12
32 ) 7,980
    -64
    158         Multiply 4 × 32
   -128         Subtract 158 - 128
    300         Compare 30 < 32
   -288         Bring down the 0.
     12         (Repeat steps.)
```
The remainder must always be less than the divisor.

Divide.

1. 46$\overline{)857}$

2. 28$\overline{)635}$

3. 32$\overline{)8,329}$

4. 55$\overline{)1,728}$

5. 21$\overline{)4,670}$

6. 17$\overline{)4,287}$

7. 58$\overline{)2,439}$

8. 73$\overline{)8,967}$

9. 91$\overline{)8,743}$

10. 52$\overline{)2,647}$

11. 37$\overline{)86,322}$

12. 48$\overline{)97,243}$

☐ I can divide up to four-digit dividends by two-digit divisors.

Solve.

S   243 × 8 = _____   D   442 × 64 = _____   T   5,432 ÷ 55 = _____

O   834 ÷ 8 = _____   W   496 ÷ 74 = _____   N   989 × 62 = _____

E   9 × 6,418 = _____   J   221 × 628 = _____   C   4,277 ÷ 18 = _____

Y   289 ÷ 72 = _____   U   2,720 ÷ 6 = _____   R   527 × 398 = _____

K   53 × 28 = _____   F   487 × 12 = _____   I   5,859 ÷ 55 = _____

A   2,566 ÷ 42 = _____   L   420 × 24 = _____   H   3,789 ÷ 16 = _____

Each person below is answering the question, "How's business?" To decode their answers, solve the problems above. Find the answers in the codes below. Write the letter of each problem above the answer. Keep solving until you have decoded all three responses.

Soldier   "Mine is

| 138,788 | 453r2 | 1,944 | 98r42 |

| 5,844 | 106r29 | 61,318 | 57,762 | , |

| 98r42 | 61r4 | 61,318 | 1,484 | 1,944 | " |

Steak House Chef   "Mine is

| 6r52 | 104r2 | 209,746 | 1,944 | 57,762 |

| 28,288 | 106r29 | 1,944 | 236r13 |

| 4r1 | 57,762 | 61r4 | 209,746 | . " |

Teacher   "Mine is   . "

| 237r11 | 10,080 | 61r4 | 1,944 | 1,944 | 4r1 |

☐ I can multiply multi-digit whole numbers.
☐ I can divide up to four-digit dividends with two-digit divisors.

Ginny took the money she earned babysitting and went to the movies. She spent **$3.90** for her ticket. Then, she spent **half** of the remaining money on popcorn. On the way home she bought an ice-cream cone for **$1.49**. When she got home, she had **$0.81** left of her earnings. How much did she earn babysitting?

$0.81	→	Start with the money left over.
+ 1.49	→	Add money spent on ice cream cone.
2.30	→	half of remaining money
+ 2.30	→	Add other half of money spent on popcorn.
4.60	→	money remaining after buying ticket
+ 3.90	→	Add money spent on ticket.
$8.50	→	**money that Ginny earned babysitting**

Solve each problem.

1. An owner of a retail clothing store bought a dress for $36.25 and sold it for $59.99. What was her profit?

2. A pair of running shoes costs $22.29. The store owner wanted to make a profit of $18.50. What should be the shoes' selling price?

3. Malcolm spent $48.74 on new speakers and $25.39 on computer games. After his purchases, he only had $0.58 left. How much money did Malcolm have before he went shopping?

4. In the town of Sleepy Oak, the fine for a speeding ticket is $32.65 + s dollars, where s is the miles per hour over the speed limit.

    A. What is the fine for going 38.4 miles per hour in a 25-miles-per-hour school zone?

    B. Mr. Taylor was fined $50.15 for speeding in the same school zone. How fast was he driving?

5. Hailey received some cash for her birthday. She spent $14.48 on a CD and donated $25.00 to charity. She put half of what was left into her savings account. She has $17.76 left. How much did she receive on her birthday?

☐ **I can solve real-world problems by adding and subtracting decimals.**

Solve each problem.

1. To make the swim team, Pedro must swim 400 meters in less than 7 minutes. Pedro swam the first 200 meters in 2.86 minutes. He swam the second 200 meters in 3.95 minutes. What is the total amount of time he took to swim 400 meters? Did Pedro make the team?

2. The school record for the 400-meter track relay was 65.5 seconds. This year's Speedsters would like to tie or break the record. It took them 53.96 seconds to run 300 meters. In how much time must they run the last 100 meters to tie the record?

3. The Whiz Kids ran the 400-meter relay in 47.35 seconds. Their time for the first 300 meters was 35.58 seconds. What was their time for the last 100 meters?

Jamie used her pedometer to keep track of how far she walked every week in July. Use the table she made to solve problems 4 to 6.

July Walking Distance in Miles	
Week 1	7.94
Week 2	13.7
Week 3	9.3
Week 4	11.25

4. Which two weeks together equal about 19 miles?

5. What is the total distance Jamie walked in July?

6. Jamie walked 21.7 miles during the month of August. How many miles did she walk in July and August combined?

7. At a track-and-field meet, the winner of the pole vault event cleared a height of 3.25 meters. This was 0.1 meters more than the height cleared by the second-place pole-vaulter. The second-place height was 0.05 meters more than the third-place height. What height did the third-place pole-vaulter clear?

8. Chang noticed a pattern in his long jump distances. So far they have been 3.2 meters, 3.35 meters, 3.5 meters, and 3.65 meters. Find Chang's pattern. What is the next distance in his pattern?

☐ **I can solve real-world problems by adding and subtracting decimals.**

Name_____

To multiply decimals, first multiply as you would with whole numbers. Then, count the total number of decimal places to the right of the decimal point in each factor. That is the number of decimal places in the product.

Examples

4.69 ← 2 decimal places	0.3 ← 1 decimal places	0.54 ← 2 decimal places
× 3 ← + 0 decimal places	×8.72 ←+ 2 decimal places	×0.38 ← + 2 decimal places
14.07 ← 2 decimal places	2.616 ← 3 decimal places	0.2052 ← 4 decimal places
↑	↑	↑
Place decimal point here.	Place decimal point here.	Place decimal point here.

Place the decimal point in each answer.

1.
$$\begin{array}{r} 199.6 \\ \times\quad 8 \\ \hline 159\,68 \end{array}$$
$$\begin{array}{r} 19.96 \\ \times\quad 8 \\ \hline 159\,68 \end{array}$$
$$\begin{array}{r} 1.996 \\ \times\quad 8 \\ \hline 159\,68 \end{array}$$
$$\begin{array}{r} 199.6 \\ \times\quad 0.8 \\ \hline 159\,68 \end{array}$$
$$\begin{array}{r} 1.996 \\ \times\quad 0.8 \\ \hline 15968 \end{array}$$

2.
$$\begin{array}{r} 300.4 \\ \times\quad 6 \\ \hline 18024 \end{array}$$
$$\begin{array}{r} 30.04 \\ \times\quad 6 \\ \hline 180\,24 \end{array}$$
$$\begin{array}{r} 3.004 \\ \times\quad 6 \\ \hline 180\,24 \end{array}$$
$$\begin{array}{r} 300.4 \\ \times\quad 0.6 \\ \hline 18024 \end{array}$$
$$\begin{array}{r} 3.004 \\ \times\quad 0.6 \\ \hline 180\,24 \end{array}$$

3.
$$\begin{array}{r} 250.2 \\ \times\quad 5 \\ \hline 1251\,0 \end{array}$$
$$\begin{array}{r} 25.02 \\ \times\quad 5 \\ \hline 125\,10 \end{array}$$
$$\begin{array}{r} 2.502 \\ \times\quad 5 \\ \hline 12510 \end{array}$$
$$\begin{array}{r} 250.2 \\ \times\quad 0.5 \\ \hline 1251\,0 \end{array}$$
$$\begin{array}{r} 2.502 \\ \times\quad 0.5 \\ \hline 12510 \end{array}$$

4.
$$\begin{array}{r} 26.4 \\ \times\quad 0.5 \\ \hline 792 \end{array}$$
$$\begin{array}{r} 42.06 \\ \times\quad 0.6 \\ \hline 2556 \end{array}$$
$$\begin{array}{r} 1\,8.7 \\ \times\quad 0.7 \\ \hline 1309 \end{array}$$
$$\begin{array}{r} 21.9 \\ \times\quad 0.4 \\ \hline 786 \end{array}$$
$$\begin{array}{r} 19.4 \\ \times\quad 3.6 \\ \hline 6984 \end{array}$$

5.
$$\begin{array}{r} 21.7 \\ \times\quad 4.2 \\ \hline 9114 \end{array}$$
$$\begin{array}{r} 63.1 \\ \times\quad 2.2 \\ \hline 13882 \end{array}$$
$$\begin{array}{r} 3\,6.6 \\ \times\quad 4.7 \\ \hline 17202 \end{array}$$
$$\begin{array}{r} 3.41 \\ \times\quad 6.2 \\ \hline 21142 \end{array}$$
$$\begin{array}{r} 7.67 \\ \times\quad 1.3 \\ \hline 9\,971 \end{array}$$

6.
$$\begin{array}{r} 21.43 \\ \times\quad 3.04 \\ \hline 651\,472 \end{array}$$
$$\begin{array}{r} 18.72 \\ \times\quad 2.17 \\ \hline 406224 \end{array}$$
$$\begin{array}{r} 24.062 \\ \times\quad 1.3 \\ \hline 312806 \end{array}$$
$$\begin{array}{r} 62.003 \\ \times\quad 1.4 \\ \hline 868042 \end{array}$$
$$\begin{array}{r} 18.417 \\ \times\quad 0.2 \\ \hline 36834 \end{array}$$

☐ **I can correctly identify the placement of the decimal point when multiplying decimals.**

Find the missing digits in the following multiplication problems. Then, place the decimal point in the product.

1.
$$
\begin{array}{r}
1\,88 \\
\times\ \boxed{1}2 \\
\hline
379 \\
+1880 \\
\hline
2256
\end{array}
$$

2.
$$
\begin{array}{r}
\boxed{\ }1\ 9 \\
\times\ 0.3\boxed{\ } \\
\hline
1038 \\
+15570 \\
\hline
2256
\end{array}
$$

3.
$$
\begin{array}{r}
8.\boxed{\ }6 \\
\times\ \boxed{\ }.3 \\
\hline
2628 \\
+35040 \\
\hline
2256
\end{array}
$$

4.
$$
\begin{array}{r}
\boxed{\ }5.6 \\
\times\ \boxed{\ }.1 \\
\hline
256 \\
+7680 \\
\hline
7936
\end{array}
$$

5.
$$
\begin{array}{r}
4.\boxed{\ }\boxed{\ } \\
\times\ 2.\boxed{\ } \\
\hline
432 \\
+8640 \\
\hline
9072
\end{array}
$$

6.
$$
\begin{array}{r}
\boxed{\ }5.6 \\
\times\ \boxed{\ }.1 \\
\hline
256 \\
+7680 \\
\hline
7936
\end{array}
$$

7.
$$
\begin{array}{r}
\boxed{\ }5.\boxed{\ } \\
\times\ \boxed{\ }.5 \\
\hline
755 \\
+6040 \\
\hline
6795
\end{array}
$$

8.
$$
\begin{array}{r}
\boxed{\ }.12 \\
\times\ 0.\boxed{\ }1 \\
\hline
312 \\
+18720 \\
\hline
19032
\end{array}
$$

❑ I can multiply decimals to the hundredths place.
❑ I can correctly identify the placement of decimal points.

Solve each problem.

Miguel is in college, studying to become a nurse. In many of his laboratory classes, he must measure quantities and record data in his notebooks.

1. Miguel performed plasma tests using 5 test tubes. Each tube contained 12.73 milliliters (mL) of plasma. How much plasma did Miguel test in total?

   He tested _____ mL total.

2. Miguel's lab partner was using a mixture of water and iodine in 8 beakers. Each beaker had 7.01 mL of the mixture in it. How much of the mixture did he have altogether?

   He had _____ mL altogether.

3. Miguel wrapped a cloth bandage around a patient's arm, turning the bandage 15 times before making it secure. He used 9.12 cm each time he turned the bandage. How long was the bandage he used?

   The bandage was about _____ cm.

4. In chemistry class, Miguel took a package of salt and split the contents evenly into 9 experimental groups. Each group weighed 0.07 kilograms (kg). How much salt was in the original package?

   There was _____ kg of salt in the original package.

5. In his dietary nutrition class, Miguel studied nutrition labels on food. According to one candy bar's label, the candy bar contained 12.4 grams of fat. If 1 gram of fat contains 9.4 calories, how many calories from fat are in the candy bar?

   There are _____ calories from fat.

6. In biology, Miguel viewed a specimen under a powerful microscope. The specimen was 0.21 cm wide. The microscope magnified the specimen 100 times larger. How wide did the specimen appear when it was viewed under the microscope?

   The specimen appeared to be _____ cm wide under the microscope.

☐ **I can solve real-world problems by multiplying decimals.**

Solve each problem.

1. A covered wagon on the Oregon Trail could travel about 2.5 miles per hour on flat terrain. About how many miles could it travel in 9 hours?

   The covered wagon could travel _____ miles.

2. Pony Express riders could carry a limited amount of weight. If a rider could carry about 1,000 letters, each weighing about 0.02 pounds, about how many pounds of letters could the Pony Express rider carry?

   The Pony Express rider could carry about _____ pounds of letters.

3. In 1860, gingham cloth sold for $0.25 a yard. Mrs. Hansen bought 16.5 yards to make clothes for her family. How much did she spend on cloth?

   Mrs. Hansen spent $_____ on cloth.

4. In 1863, travelers in Fort Laramie, Wyoming, could buy beef jerky at the trading post for $0.35 per pound. How much would a 16-pound box of jerky cost?

   A 16-pound box of jerky would cost $_____.

5. In 1838, the Hansen family traveled through Ohio by canal in 18.5 hours. The Parley Company of travelers took 2.3 times as long to go the same distance over land with their wagons. How long did it take the Parley Company?

   It took the Parley Company _____ hours to go the same distance.

6. In 1865, pioneer travelers could buy wheat for $0.12 a pound at merchant stops along the Oregon Trail. The Hansens had a barrel that could hold 19.25 pounds of wheat. How much did it cost to fill the barrel?

   It cost $_____ to fill the barrel with wheat.

7. Each wagon in the Parley Company wagon train was about 3.65 meters long. If 10 wagons traveled end to end, how long would the wagon train be?

   The wagon train would be _____ meters long.

8. If a wagon wheel travels 0.02 kilograms in one revolution, how many kilometers will the wheel have traveled after 1,190 revolutions?

   It will have traveled _____ kilometers.

☐ **I can solve real-world problems by multiplying decimals.**

Name_____

Divide **3.25 ÷ 5**

Step 1
Place the decimal point in the quotient directly above the decimal point in the dividend.

5)3.25

Remember:
The **dividend** is 3.25 because it is the number that is to be divided.

Step 2
Then, divide as you would whole numbers.

$$
\begin{array}{r}
0.65 \\
5\overline{)3.25} \\
-30 \\
\hline
25 \\
-25 \\
\hline
0
\end{array}
$$

Step 3
Check by multiplying.

$$
5\overline{)3.25}^{\,0.65}
$$

$$
\begin{array}{r}
0.65 \\
\times \quad 5 \\
\hline
3.25
\end{array}
$$

Divide. Use multiplication to check your work.

1. 8)2.4

2. 8)0.24

3. 3)0.69

4. 3)0.069

5. 2)45.4

6. 2)4.54

7. 7)$34.37

8. 5)0.15

9. 6)120.6

10. 6)12.06

11. 4)2.44

12. 6)$2.76

13. 6)5.88

14. 4)7.36

15. 8)7.52

16. 8)$10.40

17. 6)0.63

18. 8)68.28

19. 5)$543.20

20. 7)0.28

☐ I can divide decimals to the hundredths place.

Divide **2.5 ÷ 4**

Step 1 Divide the tenths.	**Step 2** Write a **0** in the hundredths place.	**Step 3** Write a **0** in the thousandths place. Bring down and divide.
$$\begin{array}{r} 0.6 \\ 4\overline{)2.5} \\ -24 \\ \hline 1 \end{array}$$	$$\begin{array}{r} 0.62 \\ 4\overline{)2.50} \\ -24 \\ \hline 10 \\ -8 \\ \hline 2 \end{array}$$ ← Write a 0 here. ← Write a 0 here. Divide by 4.	$$\begin{array}{r} 0.625 \\ 4\overline{)2.500} \\ -24 \\ \hline 10 \\ -8 \\ \hline 20 \\ -20 \\ \hline 0 \end{array}$$

Divide. Use multiplication to check your work.

1. $5\overline{)2.7}$ 2. $4\overline{)4.6}$ 3. $6\overline{)5.7}$ 4. $4\overline{)7.3}$ 5. $8\overline{)2.5}$

6. $4\overline{)0.31}$ 7. $5\overline{)8.1}$ 8. $4\overline{)6.3}$ 9. $5\overline{)0.73}$ 10. $4\overline{)4.2}$

11. $5\overline{)4.19}$ 12. $5\overline{)3.74}$ 13. $4\overline{)53.4}$ 14. $2\overline{)0.13}$ 15. $5\overline{)75.02}$

16. $18\overline{)9.63}$ 17. $40\overline{)53.6}$ 18. $16\overline{)5.2}$ 19. $32\overline{)6.8}$ 20. $56\overline{)9.8}$

☐ I can divide decimals and justify my answer using multiplication.

To divide by a decimal number, you must move the decimal to make the divisor a whole number. To make the divisor a whole number, multiply both the divisor and dividend by 10, 100, or 1,000.

Example: $0.08 \overline{)6.081}$ = $8 \overline{)608.1}$

Divide **5.44 ÷ 1.6**

Step 1

Move the decimal point one place to the right to make the divisor a whole number.

$1.6 \overline{)5.44}$ ⟵ Multiply by 10.

Step 2

Place the decimal point in the quotient. Divide as you would with whole numbers.

$$
\begin{array}{r}
3.4 \\
16 \overline{)54.4} \\
-48 \\
\hline
64 \\
-64 \\
\hline
0
\end{array}
$$

Divide. Use multiplication to check your work.

1. $0.6 \overline{)5.4}$

2. $0.9 \overline{)0.18}$

3. $1.4 \overline{)13.86}$

4. $0.8 \overline{)0.68}$

5. $1.7 \overline{)10.54}$

6. $2.4 \overline{)16.8}$

7. $0.07 \overline{)0.35}$

8. $0.02 \overline{)0.76}$

9. $0.05 \overline{)0.15}$

10. $3.2 \overline{)13.76}$

11. $0.03 \overline{)0.45}$

12. $0.8 \overline{)0.25}$

13. $0.4 \overline{)0.85}$

14. $0.08 \overline{)2.71}$

15. $0.3 \overline{)0.81}$

16. $0.6 \overline{)0.15}$

☐ I can divide decimals and justify my answer using multiplication.

Sound energy can be measured in watts. This table shows the energy output of some musical instruments.

How many snare drums would it take to produce 73.8 watts of energy?

Think: 73.8 ÷ 12.3

$$\begin{array}{r} 6 \\ 123 \overline{)\ 738} \\ -738 \\ \hline 0 \end{array}$$

So, **6** snare drums can produce 73.8 watts of energy.

Instrument	Energy Output
Piano	0.44 watts
Trombone	6.4 watts
Snare Drum	12.3 watts
Human Voice	0.000024 watts

Use the table to solve the problems.

1. How many trombones would it take to produce 1,280 watts of energy?

2. A piano can produce 8 times as much sound energy as a flute. How much energy does a flute produce?

3. About how many pianos playing together will produce the same sound energy as 1 snare drum?

4. A snare drum, a piano, and a trombone are all playing at once.
   A. What is the combined energy output of the instruments?

   B. What is the average energy output of the instruments?

5. How many pianos would produce 4.84 watts of energy?

6. A trombone can produce 80 times as much sound energy as a piccolo. What is the energy output of a piccolo?

7. What is the energy output of 1 million voices?

☐ **I can solve real-world problems by dividing decimals.**

When finding a unit cost, divide the total cost by the number of units:

$Total Cost ÷ Number of Units = $Unit Cost

or

$$\text{Number of Units} \,\overline{)\, \text{\$Total Cost}}^{\text{\$Unit Cost}}$$

Example:

Maria bought a **15**-ounce bag of tortilla chips for **$2.25.** What is the cost per ounce?

$$
\begin{array}{r}
0.15 \quad \longleftarrow \text{ Unit Cost (per ounce)} \\
\text{Number of Units} \longrightarrow 15 \,\overline{)\, 2.25} \quad \longleftarrow \text{ Total Cost} \\
-15 \\
\hline
75 \\
-75 \\
\hline
0
\end{array}
$$

So, the bag of tortilla chips cost $0.15 per ounce.

Solve each problem.

1. At Orchard Street Market, 4.5 pounds of pears cost $2.97. What is the cost per pound?

2. Mrs. Perez bought 30 ice-cream bars for her daughter's class party. She paid $12.60. How much did each ice-cream bar cost?

3. Sandra bought a 32.5-ounce package of mixed nuts for $7.15. What was the cost per ounce?

4. A $2.56 can of lemonade mix will make 64 cups of lemonade. What is the cost per cup?

5. Whole watermelons are sold for $3.99 each. Quan bought a watermelon that weighed 21 pounds. What price per pound did he pay?

6. A package of 100 napkins costs $2.00. What is the cost per napkin?

☐ **I can solve real-world problems by dividing decimals.**

To find the lowest common denominator (LCD):

1. List the multiples of each denominator.

2. The LCD is the least common multiple.

Find the LCD of $\frac{1}{4}$ and $\frac{3}{8}$. Rewrite each fraction using the LCD.

1. List the multiples of each denominator.

$4 = 4, \textcircled{8}, 12, 16, 20, 24,\ldots$

$8 = \textcircled{8}, 16, 24,\ldots$

2. The LCD = 8.

$\frac{1}{4} = \frac{}{8}$ ⟵ The LCD of 4 and 8

$\frac{1}{4} = \frac{1 \times 2}{4 \times 2} = \frac{2}{8}$

$\frac{1}{4} = \frac{2}{8}$

$\frac{3}{8} = \frac{}{8}$ ⟵ The LCD of 4 and 8

$\frac{3}{8} = \frac{3 \times 1}{8 \times 1} = \frac{3}{8}$

$\frac{3}{8} = \frac{3}{8}$

Find the lowest common denominator of each pair of fractions. Then, rewrite each fraction using the new common denominator.

1. $\frac{2}{3}, \frac{5}{6}$

2. $\frac{1}{2}, \frac{1}{4}$

3. $\frac{2}{5}, \frac{1}{10}$

4. $\frac{3}{4}, \frac{1}{12}$

5. $\frac{1}{7}, \frac{2}{14}$

6. $\frac{6}{9}, \frac{1}{3}$

7. $\frac{1}{10}, \frac{3}{5}$

8. $\frac{2}{3}, \frac{1}{2}$

9. $\frac{3}{4}, \frac{3}{5}$

☐ **I can find the lowest common denominator to replace fractions with fractions with like denominators.**

To add fractions with unlike denominators:

$$\frac{2}{3} \longrightarrow \frac{2 \times 4}{3 \times 4} \longrightarrow \frac{8}{12}$$

$$+\frac{1}{4} \longrightarrow \frac{1 \times 3}{4 \times 3} \longrightarrow \frac{3}{12}$$

$$\frac{11}{12}$$

1. Find the lowest common denominator (LCD).
2. Rewrite each fraction using the LCD.
3. Add.
4. Simplify if possible.

$$\frac{5}{6} \longrightarrow \frac{5 \times 5}{6 \times 5} \longrightarrow \frac{25}{30}$$

$$+\frac{2}{5} \longrightarrow \frac{2 \times 6}{5 \times 6} \longrightarrow \frac{12}{30}$$

$$\frac{37}{30}$$

$$= 1\frac{7}{30}$$

Add. Simplify if possible.

1. $\frac{2}{3}$
$+\frac{4}{9}$

2. $\frac{1}{4}$
$+\frac{5}{8}$

3. $\frac{3}{5}$
$+\frac{1}{10}$

4. $\frac{5}{8}$
$+\frac{1}{2}$

5. $\frac{1}{3}$
$+\frac{5}{6}$

6. $\frac{1}{5}$
$+\frac{4}{15}$

7. $\frac{1}{6}$
$+\frac{2}{3}$

8. $\frac{7}{8}$
$+\frac{3}{4}$

9. $\frac{1}{2}$
$+\frac{7}{8}$

10. $\frac{5}{8}$
$+\frac{1}{4}$

11. $\frac{6}{7}$
$+\frac{1}{14}$

12. $\frac{5}{12}$
$+\frac{5}{6}$

☐ I can use equivalent fractions to add fractions with unlike denominators.

To add fractions with unlike denominators:

$$2\frac{1}{3} \rightarrow \frac{1 \times 4}{3 \times 4} \rightarrow \frac{4}{12}$$
$$+3\frac{3}{4} \rightarrow \frac{3 \times 3}{4 \times 3} \rightarrow \frac{9}{12}$$

$$5 \qquad\qquad\qquad \frac{13}{12}$$

$$= 5 + 1\frac{1}{12} = 6\frac{1}{12}$$

1. Find the lowest common denominator (LCD).
2. Rewrite each fraction using the LCD.
3. Add.
4. Simplify if possible.

$$1\frac{7}{8} \longrightarrow \frac{7}{8}$$
$$+2\frac{1}{4} \rightarrow \frac{1 \times 2}{4 \times 2} \rightarrow \frac{2}{8}$$

$$3 \qquad\qquad\qquad \frac{9}{8}$$

$$= 3 + 1\frac{1}{8} = 4\frac{1}{8}$$

Add. Simplify if possible.

1. $1\frac{3}{8}$
   $+4\frac{1}{6}$

2. $2\frac{3}{4}$
   $+3\frac{1}{5}$

3. $5\frac{1}{3}$
   $+1\frac{5}{6}$

4. $3\frac{2}{3}$
   $+2\frac{1}{4}$

5. $6\frac{1}{2}$
   $+\ \ \frac{3}{4}$

6. $5\frac{2}{5}$
   $+2\frac{1}{3}$

7. $4\frac{1}{6}$
   $+2\frac{3}{4}$

8. $1\frac{7}{8}$
   $+2\frac{1}{6}$

9. $4\frac{5}{12}$
   $+2\frac{5}{6}$

10. $1\frac{2}{5}$
    $+3\frac{7}{10}$

11. $2\frac{3}{8}$
    $+7\frac{1}{2}$

12. $6\frac{7}{11}$
    $+5\frac{1}{2}$

❏ I can use equivalent fractions to add mixed numbers with unlike denominators.

To subtract fractions with unlike denominators:

$$\dfrac{2}{5} \longrightarrow \dfrac{2 \times 3}{5 \times 3} \longrightarrow \dfrac{6}{15}$$
$$-\dfrac{1}{3} \longrightarrow \dfrac{1 \times 5}{3 \times 5} \longrightarrow \dfrac{5}{15}$$
$$\dfrac{1}{15}$$

1. Find the lowest common denominator (LCD).
2. Rewrite each fraction using the LCD.
3. Subtract.
4. Simplify if possible.

$$\dfrac{5}{8} \longrightarrow \dfrac{5 \times 3}{8 \times 3} \longrightarrow \dfrac{15}{24}$$
$$-\dfrac{1}{3} \longrightarrow \dfrac{1 \times 3}{3 \times 8} \longrightarrow \dfrac{8}{24}$$
$$\dfrac{7}{24}$$

Subtract. Simplify if possible.

1. $\dfrac{2}{3}$ $-\dfrac{1}{4}$

2. $\dfrac{4}{5}$ $-\dfrac{1}{2}$

3. $\dfrac{1}{2}$ $-\dfrac{1}{3}$

4. $\dfrac{5}{7}$ $-\dfrac{1}{2}$

5. $\dfrac{1}{2}$ $-\dfrac{2}{9}$

6. $\dfrac{2}{3}$ $-\dfrac{2}{7}$

7. $\dfrac{3}{4}$ $-\dfrac{1}{5}$

8. $\dfrac{4}{5}$ $-\dfrac{2}{7}$

9. $\dfrac{3}{5}$ $-\dfrac{2}{9}$

10. $\dfrac{7}{8}$ $-\dfrac{2}{5}$

11. $\dfrac{5}{6}$ $-\dfrac{1}{7}$

12. $\dfrac{9}{11}$ $-\dfrac{1}{6}$

☐ I can use equivalent fractions to subtract fractions with unlike denominators.

To subtract a fraction from a whole number:

$3 \longrightarrow 2\dfrac{4}{4}$

$-\dfrac{1}{4} \longrightarrow -\dfrac{1}{4}$

$2\dfrac{3}{4}$

1. Rewrite the whole number as an equivalent fraction using the lowest common denominator (LCD).
2. Subtract.

$2 \longrightarrow 1\dfrac{6}{6}$

$-\dfrac{5}{6} \longrightarrow -\dfrac{5}{6}$

$1\dfrac{1}{6}$

Subtract.

1. $5 - \dfrac{7}{8}$

2. $3 - \dfrac{1}{3}$

3. $6 - \dfrac{7}{9}$

4. $4 - \dfrac{2}{5}$

5. $8 - \dfrac{4}{5}$

6. $5 - \dfrac{4}{9}$

7. $12 - \dfrac{3}{11}$

8. $9 - \dfrac{8}{9}$

9. $7 - \dfrac{1}{3}$

10. $10 - \dfrac{1}{5}$

11. $12 - \dfrac{7}{10}$

12. $8 - \dfrac{5}{6}$

☐ I can use equivalent fractions to rewrite whole numbers as mixed numbers.
☐ I can use equivalent fractions to subtract a fraction from a whole number.

To subtract mixed numbers:
1. Find the lowest common denominator (LCD).
2. Rewrite the fraction(s) using the LCD.
3. Rewrite again, if needed, to subtract.
4. Subtract.
5. Simplify if possible.

Steps 1 & 2

$$8\frac{1}{3} \longrightarrow 8\frac{8}{24} \longrightarrow 7\frac{32}{24}$$
$$-6\frac{5}{8} \longrightarrow 6\frac{15}{24} \longrightarrow 6\frac{15}{24}$$
$$\rule{3cm}{0.4pt}$$
$$1\frac{17}{24}$$

Step 3
$$8\frac{8}{24} = 7 + 1 + \frac{8}{24}$$
$$= 7 + \frac{24}{24} + \frac{8}{24}$$
$$= 7 + \frac{32}{24}$$

Subtract. Simplify if possible.

1. $4\frac{1}{3}$
  $-2\frac{1}{2}$

2. $6\frac{1}{8}$
  $-5\frac{1}{6}$

3. $5\frac{1}{4}$
  $-3\frac{1}{2}$

4. $8\frac{3}{5}$
  $-5\frac{1}{3}$

5. $6\frac{3}{8}$
  $-5\frac{3}{4}$

6. $4\frac{2}{9}$
  $-3\frac{2}{3}$

7. $9\frac{1}{6}$
  $-7\frac{1}{3}$

8. $5\frac{2}{5}$
  $-3\frac{7}{10}$

9. $6\frac{1}{3}$
  $-4\frac{5}{8}$

10. $7\frac{1}{4}$
  $-3\frac{7}{8}$

11. $9\frac{3}{10}$
  $-5\frac{4}{5}$

12. $3\frac{5}{12}$
  $-2\frac{2}{3}$

☐ I can use equivalent fractions to subtract mixed numbers with unlike denominators.

POOF

When you add the numbers in each row, column, and diagonal of a magic square, the sums are the same.

Find the missing numbers in each magic square. Simplify all answers.

1. The magic sum is $4\frac{1}{2}$.

$1\frac{4}{5}$		
	$1\frac{1}{2}$	
	$2\frac{9}{10}$	$1\frac{1}{5}$

2. The magic sum is 1.

$\frac{4}{15}$		$\frac{8}{15}$
	$\frac{1}{3}$	
$\frac{2}{15}$		$\frac{2}{5}$

3. The magic sum is $3\frac{15}{16}$.

$1\frac{1}{8}$		$1\frac{3}{8}$
$1\frac{1}{4}$		$1\frac{1}{2}$

4. The magic sum is $6\frac{5}{6}$.

$2\frac{1}{3}$		$2\frac{4}{9}$
$2\frac{1}{9}$		$2\frac{2}{9}$

☐ I can add and subtract fractions with unlike denominators.

Use the information in the recipe to solve each problem.
Write the answer in simplest form.

> **Trail Mix Recipe**
>
> $1\frac{1}{4}$ cups sunflower seeds
>
> $1\frac{1}{2}$ cups peanuts
>
> $\frac{3}{4}$ cup candy-coated chocolate pieces
>
> $\frac{5}{8}$ cup raisins
>
> (Makes 1 batch)

1. Mrs. Johnson plans to make a batch of trail mix, and she would like to add extra raisins. If she doubles the amount of raisins in the recipe, how many cups of raisins will she need?

2. After measuring the amount of peanuts needed to make a batch of trail mix, Mrs. Johnson had $2\frac{1}{2}$ cups of peanuts left over. How many cups of peanuts did she begin with?

3. Ellen Johnson increased the amount of candy-coated chocolate pieces in the recipe to $1\frac{1}{8}$ cups. How many more cups of chocolate pieces did she use than the recipe required?

4. If none of the measurements are altered, how many cups of trail mix does one batch make when all of the ingredients are added together?

5. The Johnson family made enough trail mix to take on their hike. They hiked $4\frac{3}{8}$ miles to Green River Gulch and then walked another $1\frac{9}{16}$ miles down the riverbank. How far did they hike altogether?

6. Sam and Ellen Johnson hiked an extra $\frac{18}{5}$ miles on an advanced trail. Write the extra distance they hiked as a mixed number.

> ☐ **I can add and subtractions fractions to solve real-world problems.**

Solve each problem.

1. In a baseball game, the starting pitcher pitched 5 innings. The relief pitcher pitched another $1\frac{2}{3}$ innings before the closing pitcher came in to finish the game.

   A. How many more innings did the starting pitcher pitch than the relief pitcher?

   B. How many innings had the closing pitcher pitched after he finished the ninth inning?

2. In a city baseball league, the Tigers are $1\frac{1}{2}$ games behind the Pirates, and the Pirates are 4 games ahead of the Cubs. How many games separate the Tigers and the Cubs?

3. Softball bats are $2\frac{1}{2}$ inches in diameter. If a softball is $3\frac{1}{8}$ inches in diameter, how much wider is the softball than the bat?

4. Suppose $\frac{5}{8}$ of major league baseball fans watch the games on television, and $\frac{1}{3}$ of the fans listen to them on the radio. How many more baseball fans watch television than listen to the radio? Write your answer as a fraction.

5. Bob spent $\frac{3}{8}$ of his birthday money at a baseball game and $\frac{5}{12}$ on a new bat and glove. What fraction of his birthday money did Bob spend?

6. If a baseball game lasted $3\frac{1}{4}$ hours and ended at 10 pm, at what time did it start?

☐ **I can add and subtractions fractions to solve real-world problems.**

Name_____

Read the scenario. Then, answer each question. Check the answer for reasonableness.

Four classmates, Rachel, Greg, Ethan, and Sarah, are competing in an obstacle course. The course is 1 mile long. Each person must complete one part of the competition. The course begins with running through tires for $\frac{1}{6}$ mile, dribbling a basketball for $\frac{1}{4}$ mile, running $\frac{1}{2}$ mile, and then crossing the monkey bars.

1. If Rachel runs through the tires for $\frac{1}{6}$ of a mile and Greg dribbles the basketball for $\frac{1}{4}$ mile, what fraction of the course have Rachel and Greg completed?

2. A. If Ethan then runs for $\frac{1}{2}$ mile, how much of the course have Rachel, Greg, and Ethan completed?

   B. What fraction of the 1-mile course must Sarah cross on the monkey bars?

3. A. What fraction of the course did the boys, Greg and Ethan, cover?

   B. What fraction did the girls, Rachel and Sarah, cover?

4. The team took 25 minutes to complete the race. If Rachel took $5\frac{1}{4}$ minutes, Greg took $7\frac{1}{4}$ minutes, and Sarah took $6\frac{1}{6}$ minutes, how long did it take Ethan to run the $\frac{1}{2}$ mile?

☐ I can add and subtract fractions to solve real-world problems.
☐ I can use my understanding of fractions to decide if my answers are reasonable.

Use the table to solve each problem. Write the answer in simplest form. Check the answer for reasonableness.

Jobs	Tasha's Time per Job	Tyrone's Time per Job
Homework	$2\frac{1}{4}$ hours	$1\frac{2}{3}$ hours
Clean bathroom	$\frac{3}{4}$ hour	$\frac{1}{2}$ hour
Clean bedroom	$\frac{1}{3}$ hour	1 hour
Walk dog	$\frac{1}{2}$ hour	$\frac{3}{4}$ hour

1. How much total time does it take both Tasha and Tyrone to do their homework?

2. How much more time does Tasha spend on her homework than Tyrone?

3. How much more time does Tyrone spend cleaning his bedroom than Tasha?

4. If Tyrone comes home from school, does his homework, and then walks the dog, how much time will it take him?

5. If Tasha cleans once a week, how much time does she spend cleaning the bathroom and bedroom per week?

6. If Tyrone cleans the bathroom two times a week and Tasha cleans the bathroom only once a week, who spends more time cleaning the bathroom?

☐ I can solve word problems by adding and subtracting fractions with like and unlike denominators.
☐ I can use my understanding of fractions to decide if my answers are reasonable.

Use division to change each improper fraction into a whole number.

$\frac{14}{3}$ can be rewritten as $14 \div 3$ or $3\overline{)14}$.

$\frac{14}{3}$ is an improper fraction.

$\begin{array}{r} 4r2 \\ 3\overline{)14} \\ -12 \\ \hline 2 \end{array}$ $\frac{14}{3} = 4\frac{2}{3}$

$4\frac{2}{3}$ is a mixed number.

The numerator becomes 2; the denominator stays 3.

1. $\frac{15}{2}$

2. $\frac{7}{4}$

3. $\frac{20}{7}$

4. $\frac{43}{5}$

5. $\frac{23}{8}$

6. $\frac{21}{5}$

7. $\frac{31}{12}$

8. $\frac{5}{2}$

9. $\frac{13}{8}$

10. $\frac{11}{4}$

11. $\frac{49}{9}$

12. $\frac{41}{6}$

13. $\frac{23}{3}$

14. $\frac{45}{4}$

15. $\frac{60}{5}$

16. $\frac{23}{7}$

17. $\frac{72}{6}$

18. $\frac{16}{2}$

☐ **I can explain that a fraction is the division of the numerator by the denominator.**

Solve each problem. Leave your answer as a fraction or mixed number in simplified form.

1. Cindy baked 2 apple pies for herself and 7 other friends. If she divides the pies evenly among the 8 people, what fraction of pie will each person get?

2. Chang has 16 cups of cake batter, and he plans to divide it evenly to make 24 cupcakes. How many cups of batter will be in each cupcake?

3. Dominique needs 6 cups of dog food to feed her 4 dogs. If each dog gets the same amount of food, how many cups of food does each dog eat?

4. Gabe needs to cut an 8-foot piece of plywood into 16 equivalent pieces for a fence. How wide will each piece be if all are the same length?

5. A baker purchases flour in 25-pound bags and then separates it equally into 4 containers for storage. How many pounds of flour are in each container?

6. Dylan uses 4 cups of shredded cheese on 3 pizzas. How many cups of cheese are on each pizza?

☐ I can solve division word problems where the answer will be a fraction or a mixed number.

Name_____

Visualize $\frac{1}{2}$ × $\frac{1}{4}$ as

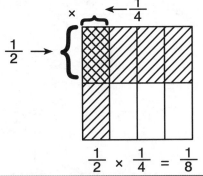

$$\frac{1}{2} \times \frac{1}{4} = \frac{1}{8}$$

Visualize $\frac{2}{3}$ × $\frac{4}{5}$ as

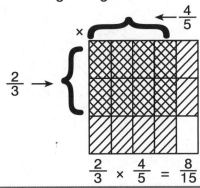

$$\frac{2}{3} \times \frac{4}{5} = \frac{8}{15}$$

Multiply using the visual fraction model.

1.

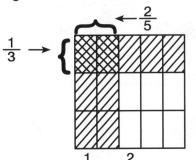

$$\frac{1}{3} \times \frac{2}{5} = \underline{\quad}$$

2.

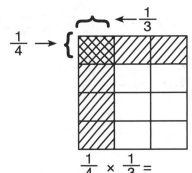

$$\frac{1}{4} \times \frac{1}{3} = \underline{\quad}$$

3.

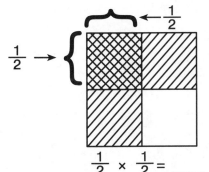

$$\frac{1}{2} \times \frac{1}{2} = \underline{\quad}$$

4.

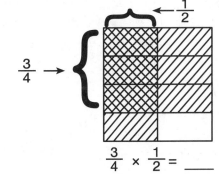

$$\frac{3}{4} \times \frac{1}{2} = \underline{\quad}$$

5.

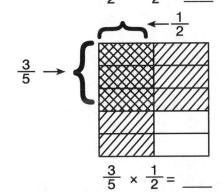

$$\frac{3}{5} \times \frac{1}{2} = \underline{\quad}$$

6.

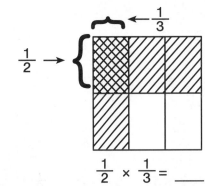

$$\frac{1}{2} \times \frac{1}{3} = \underline{\quad}$$

☐ I can use a visual representation to multiply fractions.

Name_____

When multiplying $\frac{1}{2} \times \frac{1}{4}$:

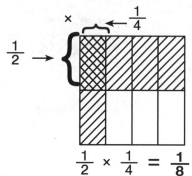

$\frac{1}{2} \times \frac{1}{4} = \frac{1}{8}$

Multiply the numerators.
Multiply the denominators.

$\frac{1}{2} \times \frac{1}{4} = \frac{1}{2} \frac{\times\ 1}{\times\ 4} = \frac{1}{8}$

$\frac{3}{4} \times \frac{1}{7} = \frac{1}{4} \frac{\times\ 3}{\times\ 7} = \frac{3}{28}$

Multiply. Simplify if possible.

1. $\frac{1}{2} \times \frac{3}{4} =$ 2. $\frac{2}{3} \times \frac{1}{5} =$ 3. $\frac{2}{5} \times \frac{1}{3} =$ 4. $\frac{5}{6} \times \frac{1}{2} =$

5. $\frac{1}{4} \times \frac{3}{8} =$ 6. $\frac{5}{12} \times \frac{1}{2} =$ 7. $\frac{1}{2} \times \frac{5}{7} =$ 8. $\frac{1}{3} \times \frac{1}{4} =$

9. $\frac{1}{5} \times \frac{2}{5} =$ 10. $\frac{3}{5} \times \frac{1}{2} =$ 11. $\frac{3}{4} \times \frac{3}{5} =$ 12. $\frac{3}{4} \times \frac{1}{8} =$

13. $\frac{2}{5} \times \frac{3}{5} =$ 14. $\frac{1}{2} \times \frac{1}{2} =$ 15. $\frac{2}{3} \times \frac{2}{3} =$ 16. $\frac{3}{8} \times \frac{1}{2} =$

17. $\frac{5}{7} \times \frac{1}{3} =$ 18. $\frac{1}{2} \times \frac{3}{7} =$ 19. $\frac{5}{8} \times \frac{1}{3} =$ 20. $\frac{5}{6} \times \frac{1}{3} =$

21. $\frac{3}{5} \times \frac{1}{7} =$ 22. $\frac{1}{8} \times \frac{1}{2} =$ 23. $\frac{1}{4} \times \frac{3}{7} =$ 24. $\frac{5}{9} \times \frac{1}{2} =$

☐ I can multiply fractions using various strategies.

$2\frac{1}{4} \times 1\frac{1}{2} = \frac{9 \times 3}{4 \times 2}$

$= \frac{9 \times 3}{4 \times 2}$

$= \frac{27}{8}$

$= 3\frac{3}{8}$

When multiplying mixed numbers:
1. Rewrite the numbers as improper fractions.
2. Multiply the numerators.
3. Multiply the denominators.
4. Simplify if possible.

$1\frac{1}{3} \times 2\frac{1}{8} = \frac{4 \times 17}{3 \times 8}$

$= \frac{4 \times 17}{3 \times 8}$

$= \frac{68}{24}$

$= 2\frac{20}{24} = 2\frac{5}{6}$

Multiply. Simplify if possible.

1. $3\frac{3}{4} \times 2\frac{2}{3} =$

2. $1\frac{1}{4} \times 2\frac{1}{2} =$

3. $2\frac{1}{5} \times 2\frac{1}{4} =$

4. $1\frac{1}{5} \times 2\frac{1}{6} =$

5. $1\frac{3}{5} \times 1\frac{2}{5} =$

6. $2\frac{1}{2} \times 3\frac{1}{3} =$

7. $4\frac{1}{2} \times 1\frac{2}{3} =$

8. $2\frac{4}{5} \times 5\frac{1}{4} =$

9. $2\frac{3}{8} \times 2\frac{1}{3} =$

10. $1\frac{4}{5} \times 1\frac{1}{4} =$

11. $1\frac{3}{7} \times 1\frac{3}{8} =$

12. $1\frac{1}{2} \times 3\frac{2}{3} =$

13. $4\frac{1}{2} \times 1\frac{2}{5} =$

14. $2\frac{2}{3} \times 3\frac{1}{2} =$

15. $4\frac{1}{2} \times 1\frac{1}{2} =$

16. $2\frac{3}{8} \times 3\frac{2}{7} =$

☐ **I can multiply mixed numbers.**

Name_____

Answer each question.

1. If you multiply 6 by $\frac{1}{4}$, will your answer be greater or less than 6? How do you know?

2. If you multiply 8 by $\frac{5}{4}$, will your answer be greater or less than 8? How do you know?

3. If you multiply $\frac{3}{4}$ by 7, will your answer be greater or less than 7? How do you know?

4. If you multiply $\frac{5}{2}$ by 4, will your answer be greater or less than 4? How do you know?

5. A drawing has dimensions of 9 inches by 12 inches. If you want the drawing scaled down to fit a 3 inch by 4 inch frame, by what fraction would you multiply the dimensions?

6. A picture has dimensions of 5 cm by 10 cm. If you want to enlarge the picture to a size of $32\frac{1}{2}$ cm by 65 cm, by what fraction would you multiply the dimensions?

7. A quilt pattern makes a quilt that is 48 inches by 60 inches. If you want to make the quilt $\frac{1}{3}$ smaller, how would you find the new dimensions? What would the new dimensions be?

☐ I can understand multiplication by comparing the sizes of the factors.
☐ I can solve real world problems that involve scaling with fractions.

Solve each problem. Write the answer in simplified form.

1. Cody is making dinner for a group of his friends. He is making a recipe for stuffed chilies that uses $1\frac{3}{4}$ cups of cream cheese. Cody will only need to make $\frac{2}{3}$ of the recipe. How much cream cheese should he use?

2. A 2-serving recipe for chicken mole calls for $\frac{3}{12}$ teaspoons of chili powder and $1\frac{1}{2}$ tablespoons of olive oil. How much of each ingredient is needed to make 3 servings?

3. Cody has $\frac{7}{8}$ pound of cheese. He uses $\frac{1}{7}$ of this in his quesadillas. Since there are 16 ounces in 1 pound, how many ounces of cheese does Cody use in his quesadillas?

Solve problems 4–6 using this recipe.

Chilaquillas (Serves 6)	
1 dozen tortillas	$\frac{2}{3}$ cup chopped green onions
$2\frac{1}{2}$ cups grated jack cheese	$2\frac{1}{4}$ teaspoons chili powder
$1\frac{1}{3}$ cups tomato sauce	$\frac{1}{2}$ teaspoon crushed oregano
$1\frac{1}{4}$ cups low fat cottage cheese	$\frac{1}{4}$ cup oil

4. Cody will need enough chilaquillas to serve 8 people. By what number should the recipe be multiplied to make enough for all 8 people?

5. How much tomato sauce is required if the recipe is multiplied by $1\frac{1}{3}$?

6. How many cups of chopped green onions will be needed if the recipe is tripled?

7. Cody's recipe instructs him to bake at 205°C. He can convert this temperature to degrees Fahrenheit (°F) using this formula:

$$°F = \frac{9}{5} \times °C + 32$$

What cooking temperature should he use in degrees Fahrenheit?

☐ I can multiply fractions to solve real-world problems.

Solve each problem. Write the answer in simplified form.

1. Austin is going to the movie theater. It is $3\frac{3}{5}$ miles from his house. Austin decides to take his motor scooter, but it breaks down $\frac{2}{3}$ of the way there. How far is Austin from his house?

2. Austin's motor scooter uses $\frac{1}{4}$ of a gallon of fuel for each mile. How much fuel has he used?

3. Austin purchases $\frac{2}{3}$ of a pound of yum-yum treats. If yum-yum treats are $6.00 per pound, how much does Austin pay?

4. In the theater, Austin meets his friends, who have purchased a gigantic barrel of popcorn. Only $\frac{3}{4}$ of it is left. Austin eats $\frac{1}{3}$ of the remaining popcorn. How much of the barrel did Austin eat?

5. After the movie, Austin starts walking home. He walks $\frac{1}{6}$ of the $3\frac{3}{5}$ miles to his house before his mom picks him up. How far does Austin walk?

☐ I can solve real-world problems by multiplying fractions and mixed numbers.

Solve each problem. Write the answer in simplified form.

1. Jamaica's class has 24 students. If $\frac{1}{8}$ of them play the piano, how many students in her class play the piano?

2. There are 12 students working in the library. If $\frac{3}{4}$ of them are girls, how many girls are in the library?

3. In the library, 6 students are working on math. Of those 6 students, $\frac{2}{3}$ of them are working on fractions. How many students are working on fractions?

4. Jamaica spent half of her $1\frac{1}{2}$-hour gym class jumping rope. How long did she spend jumping rope?

5. Jamaica's class spent $1\frac{3}{4}$ hours in science class. They studied insects for $\frac{2}{3}$ of the time. How much time did she spend studying insects?

☐ I can solve real-world problems by multiplying fractions and mixed numbers.

During Year 2, the size of a pond decreases to $\frac{1}{3}$ of what it was in Year 1. Assume that the same decrease occurs during Year 3. What fraction of the pond will remain after Year 3?

Picture It

Here is a model of the information.

Year 1

Year 2

Year 3

Solve It

Use the model to help you solve the problem.

Let 1 represent the whole pond in Year 1.

After Year 2 the pond is $\frac{1}{3}$ the size of Year 1.
Find the fraction of the pond remaining after Year 2.

$\frac{1}{3} \times 1 = \frac{1}{3}$

After Year 3 the pond is $\frac{1}{3}$ the size of Year 2.
Find the fraction of the pond remaining after Year 3.

$\frac{1}{3} \times \frac{1}{3} = \frac{1}{9}$

After Year 3, the pond will be $\frac{1}{9}$ the size it was in Year 1.

Solve each problem. Draw a model to help you.

1. Suppose every bounce of a ball is $\frac{2}{3}$ the height of its previous bounce. What fraction of the original height will the height of Bounce 3 be?

   Bounce 1

   Bounce 2

   Bounce 3

   On Bounce 3, the ball will bounce to _____ of its original height.

2. Suppose a ball is dropped from its original height of 2 meters. Every bounce of the ball is $\frac{1}{2}$ the height of its previous bounce. How high will the ball bounce on Bounce 3?

   On Bounce 3, the ball will bounce _____ meter high.

3. A different ball is dropped from a height of 10 meters. On each bounce, it reaches $\frac{4}{5}$ of the height of its previous bounce. How high will the ball bounce on its third bounce?

   The ball will bounce _____ meters high on its third bounce.

☐ I can use a model to solve fraction word problems.

When dividing fractions and whole numbers, first rename the whole number as a fraction with a denominator of 1.

To divide a fraction by a whole number:

Divide $\frac{4}{5} \div 8$

$\frac{4}{5} \div 8 = \frac{4}{5} \div \frac{8}{1}$ Write the whole number as a fraction with a denominator of 1.

$= \frac{4}{5} \times \frac{1}{8}$ Multiply $\frac{4}{5}$ by the reciprocal of $\frac{8}{1}$.

$= \frac{4 \times 1}{5 \times 8}$

$= \frac{4}{40}$

$= \frac{1}{10}$ Reduce the answer to the lowest terms.

To divide a whole number by a fraction:

Divide $5 \div \frac{3}{4}$

$5 \div \frac{3}{4} = \frac{5}{1} \div \frac{3}{4}$ Write the whole number as a fraction with a denominator of 1.

$= \frac{5}{1} \times \frac{4}{3}$ Multiply $\frac{5}{1}$ by the reciprocal of $\frac{3}{4}$.

$= \frac{5 \times 4}{1 \times 3}$

$= \frac{20}{3}$

$= 6\frac{2}{3}$ Change improper fractions to mixed numbers.

Divide. Write each quotient in its simplest form.

1. $6 \div \frac{4}{9} =$

2. $5 \div \frac{1}{7} =$

3. $\frac{4}{7} \div 8 =$

4. $\frac{6}{5} \div 2 =$

5. $\frac{3}{5} \div 4 =$

6. $\frac{5}{8} \div 5 =$

7. $\frac{9}{10} \div 4 =$

8. $\frac{1}{6} \div 3 =$

9. $\frac{9}{4} \div 6 =$

10. $\frac{5}{3} \div 4 =$

11. $\frac{4}{3} \div 5 =$

12. $\frac{8}{5} \div 5 =$

13. $\frac{10}{9} \div 4 =$

14. $\frac{7}{4} \div 3 =$

15. $8 \div \frac{2}{3} =$

16. $10 \div \frac{4}{5} =$

☐ I can divide a whole number by a fraction.
☐ I can divide a fraction by a whole number.

Draw a line to match each scenario to the correct division problem. Then, solve.

1. How many pieces of rope will you have if you cut a 2-foot piece of rope into $\frac{1}{4}$-foot sections?

A. $3\frac{1}{2} \div 7$

2. Jennifer has $3\frac{1}{2}$ cups of jelly beans to share with 7 friends. How many cups does each person get?

B. $7 \div 3\frac{1}{2}$

3. Nadia made 4 cups of tea. She wants to pour it into glasses that each hold $\frac{1}{2}$ cup. How many glasses will she fill?

C. $2 \div \frac{1}{4}$

4. Demetri needs to make 7 cups of coffee for his family's breakfast, but his coffee pot only makes $3\frac{1}{2}$ cups at a time. How many pots of coffee must he make to serve everyone?

D. $\frac{1}{4} \div 2$

5. Blake and Jerome will split $\frac{1}{4}$ of a cherry pie. How much of the cherry pie will each get?

E. $4 \div \frac{1}{2}$

6. Ella has $\frac{1}{2}$ teaspoon of salt left. If the salt must last 4 days, how much salt can she use each day?

F. $\frac{1}{2} \div 4$

☐ I can solve real-world problems by dividing fractions and whole numbers.

Solve each problem.

1. A box contains 10 ounces of cereal. If one serving is $1\frac{1}{4}$ ounces, how many servings are in the box?

   There are _____ servings in the cereal box.

2. A can of soup contains $22\frac{3}{4}$ ounces. If one can contains $3\frac{1}{2}$ servings of soup, how many ounces are in one serving?

   There are _____ ounces of soup in one serving.

3. Ten melons weigh $17\frac{1}{2}$ pounds. What is the average weight of each melon?

   The average weight of each melon is _____ pounds.

4. Chrissie bought $\frac{3}{4}$ pound of grapes to put in her bag lunches. If she eats the same amount each day and finishes the grapes in 5 days, how much does she eat each day?

   She eats _____ ounces of grapes each day.

5. Mrs. Walker bought $5\frac{1}{2}$ feet of licorice to share equally between her 5 children and herself. How many feet of licorice will each person receive? How many inches of licorice will each person receive?

   Each person will receive _____ feet, or _____ inches, of licorice.

6. Mrs. Walker bought a 35-ounce package of flour. She used $\frac{1}{3}$ of it to bake 5 loaves of bread. How many ounces of flour were in each loaf of bread?

   There are _____ ounces of flour in each loaf of bread.

7. Mrs. Walker bought a $2\frac{3}{4}$-pound roast for their family dinner. A total of 9 people will be at the dinner. How many ounces of roast will each person get if the roast is divided equally?

   Each person will get _____ ounces of roast.

☐ **I can solve real-world problems by dividing fractions.**

Solve each problem. Write the answer as a simplified fraction.

1. A 6-foot submarine sandwich is cut into $\frac{1}{6}$ foot pieces for serving. How many smaller sandwiches can be made out of the long party sub?

2. Grace is making chocolate chip cookies using a recipe that calls for $\frac{3}{4}$ cup of sugar. If Grace has 3 cups of sugar, how many batches of cookies can she make?

3. Lamar has $4\frac{1}{2}$ cups of juice to split between 12 people How many cups of juice will each person receive?

Write a word problem for each division problem.

4. $6 \div \frac{1}{2}$

_____

_____

_____

5. $\frac{3}{4} \div 4$

_____

_____

_____

☐ I can solve real-world problems by dividing fractions and whole numbers.
☐ I can write word problems for given division problems.

5.NF.2, 5.NF.4, 5.NF.7

Solve each problem. Write the answer in simplified form.

1. A bag of jelly beans contains $\frac{1}{2}$ cup of red jelly beans, $\frac{2}{3}$ cup of blue jelly beans, and $\frac{1}{4}$ cup of yellow jelly beans. How many total cups of jelly beans are in the bag?

2. A pitcher contains $4\frac{1}{2}$ cups of juice. If Derek pours $\frac{3}{4}$ cup into a glass, how much juice is left in the pitcher?

3. One lap around the track is $\frac{1}{4}$ mile. If Hector runs $\frac{2}{3}$ of a lap, what fraction of a mile did he run?

4. A relay race requires runners to run a total distance of 2 miles. If each runner is responsible for running $\frac{1}{2}$ mile, how many runners are needed to run the entire race?

5. Caroline made a pizza for her family. Her dad ate $\frac{1}{4}$ of the pizza. The rest of the pizza was split evenly among the 3 remaining family members. What fraction of the pizza did each remaining family member eat?

☐ **I can solve real-world problems by adding, subtracting, multiplying, and dividing fractions.**

Name_____

Solve each problem. Write the answer in simplified form.

1. Of the 40 students who auditioned for the school play, $\frac{3}{4}$ of them were called back for a second audition. Of those called back, only $\frac{1}{3}$ received a part in the play. What fraction of those students who auditioned actually received a part in the play?

2. The main song in the play is a duet that is $2\frac{1}{2}$ minutes long. If the 2 singers get equal singing time, how many minutes does each sing?

3. The curtain on the stage is $15\frac{1}{2}$ feet tall, which is $\frac{1}{4}$ foot too short to hide all of the props. How tall does the curtain need to be to hide all of the props?

4. The entire play is $1\frac{3}{4}$ hours long, which is evenly divided among 3 acts. How long is each act?

5. The audience was composed of parents and students. There were 84 people enjoying the show. If $\frac{1}{3}$ of the audience was parents, how many students attended the play?

☐ I can solve real-world problems adding, subtracting, multiplying, and dividing fractions.

The chart shows the relationship between units of length in the customary measurement system.

Divide to change a smaller unit to a larger unit.
51 feet = ___ yards
Think: 3 ft. = 1 yd.
51 ÷ 3 = 17
51 ft. = 17 yd.

Units of Length	
12 inches (in.)	= 1 foot (ft.)
3 feet	= 1 yard (yd.)
36 inches	= 1 yard
5,280 feet	= 1 mile (mi.)
1,760 yards	= 1 mile

Multiply to change a larger unit to a smaller unit.
6 yards = ___ inches
Think: 1 yd. = 36 in.
6 × 36 = 216
6 yd. = 216 in.

Circle the greater length.

1. 10 in. or 1 ft.

2. 3 ft. or 38 in.

3. 1 ft. 7 in. or 17 in.

4. 4 ft. 4 in. or 56 in.

5. 1 ft. 9 in. or 2 ft.

6. 7 ft. or 2 yd.

7. 6 yd. or 17 ft.

8. 26 in. or 2 ft.

9. 5 ft. or $1\frac{1}{2}$ yd.

10. 110 in. or 3 yd.

11. 5,000 ft. or 1 mi.

12. 1,000 ft. or 2 mi.

13. 5,000 yd. or 3 mi.

14. 7,020 ft. or 4 mi.

15. 3,200 yd. or 2 mi.

Write the equivalent measure.

16. 6 ft. = _____ in.

17. 72 in. = _____ yd.

18. 2 mi. = _____ yd.

19. 24 in. = _____ ft.

20. 18 ft. = _____ yd.

21. $1\frac{1}{2}$ ft. = _____ in.

22. 12 in. = _____ yd.

23. 2 mi. = _____ ft.

24. 1 ft. 3 in. = _____ n.

25. 1 yd. 11 in. = _____ in.

26. 4 yd. = _____ ft.

27. $\frac{2}{3}$ yd. = _____ ft.

28. 60 in. = _____ ft.

29. 5,280 yd. = _____ mi.

30. 10 yd. = _____ in.

31. 10 mi. = _____ yd.

32. 8 ft. 12 in. = _____ yd.

33. 1 mi. = _____ ft.

☐ **I can convert units within a measurement system.**

The amount of liquid a container can hold can be measured by using units such as the cup and the quart.

Many of the bottled liquids you buy in the store are measured in fluid ounces (fl. oz.). There are 8 fluid ounces in a cup, 16 fluid ounces in a pint, 32 fluid ounces in a quart, and 128 fluid ounces in a gallon.

Units of Capacity

8 fluid ounces (fl. oz.)	= 1 cup
2 cups	= 1 pint (pt.)
16 fluid ounces	= 1 pint
2 pints	= 1 quart (qt.)
4 quarts	= 1 gallon (gal.)

Examples:

32 fl. oz. = _?_ cups
Think: 1 cup = 8 fl. oz. To change from a smaller unit to a larger unit, divide.
32 ÷ 8 = 4   32 fl. oz. = 4 cups

5 qt. = _?_ pt.
Think: 1 qt. = 2 pt. To change from a larger unit to a smaller unit, multiply.
5 × 2 = 10
5 qt. = 10 pt.

Choose the most reasonable unit of measure for each. Write *fl. oz., cup, pt., qt.,* or *gal.*

1. a canned soft drink _____   a pitcher of juice _____   a sip of water _____

2. the water in a bathtub _____   the amount of sugar in a cake recipe _____

Write the equivalent measure.

3. 1 qt. = _____ pt.

4. 32 fl. oz. = _____ cups

5. 2 cups = _____ pt.

6. 16 fl. oz. = _____ pt.

7. 3 gal. = _____ qt.

8. 1 pt. = _____ fl. oz.

9. $\frac{1}{2}$ gal. = _____ cups

10. $\frac{1}{2}$ gal. = _____ pt.

11. $\frac{1}{2}$ gal. = _____ qt.

12. 3 qt. = _____ pt.

13. 4 pt. = _____ gal.

14. 1 gal. = _____ fl. oz.

15. 8 gal. = _____ qt.

16. 12 qt. = _____ gal.

17. 22 pt. = _____ qt.

Compare using <, >, or =.

18. 10 fl. oz. ◯ 1 cup

19. 5 qt. ◯ 2 gal.

20. 2 cups ◯ 46 fl. oz.

21. 64 fl. oz. ◯ 2 qt.

22. 3 gal. ◯ 22 pt.

23. 12 pt. ◯ 3 gal.

24. 160 fl. oz. ◯ 10 pt.

25. 100 fl. oz. ◯ 10 cups

26. 100 qt. ◯ 125 gal.

☐ **I can convert measurement units within a measurement system.**

Name_____

The basic unit of weight in the customary measurement system is the pound.
• Four sticks of butter weigh 1 **pound**.
• A large truck weighs about 2 **tons**.

Example: 64 oz. = _?_ lb.
Think: 1 lb. = 16 oz.
$64 \div 16 = 4$
64 oz. = 4 lb.

Units of Weight
16 ounces (oz.) = 1 pound (lb.)
2,000 pounds = 1 ton

Write the equivalent weight.

1. 96 oz. = _____ lb.

2. 3 lb. = _____ oz.

3. 7 tons = _____ lb.

4. 1 ton = _____ oz.

5. 160 oz. =_____ lb.

6. 10,000 lb. = _____ tons

7. 16 lb. 5 oz. = _____ oz.

8. 9 lb. 3 oz. = _____ oz.

9. $2\frac{1}{2}$ tons = _____ lb.

Compare using <, >, or =.

10. 96 oz. $\bigcirc$ 20 lb.

11. 80 oz. $\bigcirc$ 6 lb.

12. 3 lb. $\bigcirc$ 50 oz.

13. $1\frac{1}{2}$ tons $\bigcirc$ 3,000 lb.

14. 320 oz. $\bigcirc$ 10 lb.

15. 61 oz. $\bigcirc$ 4 lb.

16. 82 oz. $\bigcirc$ 5 lb.

17. 6 tons $\bigcirc$ 10,000 lb.

18. 100 oz. $\bigcirc$ 7 lb.

19. $\frac{1}{2}$ ton $\bigcirc$ 1,000 lb.

20. 32,000 oz. $\bigcirc$ 1 ton

21. 1,600 oz. $\bigcirc$ 100 lb.

Solve each problem.

22. Shannon uses 30 inches of ribbon to make one bow. How many feet of ribbon are needed to make 10 bows?

23. At the end of a bike ride, everyone drank a 16-fluid ounce bottle of sports drink. If 12 kids and 2 adults were on the bike ride, how many quarts of sports drink did the riders drink?

24.   How many pounds of nails will be needed to fill 100 boxes with 8 oz. of nails in each?

☐ **I can convert measurement units within a measurement system.**

Name_____

Solve each problem.

1. Alexis bought 1 gallon of milk. She had a recipe that called for 1 quart of milk. After making the recipe, how many quarts of milk does she have left?

2. Jake has 1 pound of cheese. He puts 6 ounces onto a pizza he is making. How many ounces of cheese does he have left?

3. Khalil bought a pint of ice cream. How many cups of ice cream does he have?

4. Gabriel ran for 1 mile. Then, he started jogging. He jogged for 250 feet. How many total feet did he run and jog?

5. A football field is 100 yards long. How many feet is that?

6. Kade purchased 2 gallons of chocolate milk. Malia purchased 6 quarts of chocolate milk.

   A. How many quarts of chocolate milk did Kade purchase?

   B. Who has more chocolate milk?

   C. How much more chocolate milk??

7. Derek has 2 feet of Tasty Cherry Rope. He plans on splitting it evenly between himself and 5 of his friends.

   A. How many inches of Tasty Cherry Rope does Derek have?

   B. How many inches should each person get?

8. India has 3 pounds of jelly beans. If she gives 4 ounces to each person, how many people can she give her jelly beans to?

☐ I can convert measurement units within a measurement system.
☐ I can use converted measurements to solve real-world problems.

> 1 kilometer (km) = 1,000 meters (m)
> 1 meter (m) = 100 centimeters (cm)
> 1 centimeter (cm) = 10 millimeters (mm)

5 m = _____ cm
Think: 1 m = 100 cm
So, 5 m = 5 × 100 cm
5 m = **500 cm**

72,000 m = _____ km
Think: 1,000 m = 1 km
So, 72,000 m = (72,000 ÷ 1,000) km
72,000 m = **72 km**

520 mm = _____ cm
Think: 10 mm = 1 cm
So, 520 mm = (520 ÷ 10) cm
520 mm = **52 cm**

Write the equivalent measure.

1. 42 m = _____ cm

2. 620 mm = _____ cm

3. 4 km = _____ m

4. 8,000 m = _____ km

5. 85 cm = _____ mm

6. 5,400 mm = _____ cm

7. If Kayleigh is 102 centimeters tall, is she greater than or less than 1 meter tall?

8. Your dresser is 196 centimeters wide. Will it fit along a wall that is 2 meters long?

9. Dylan has a roll of wrapping paper that is 5 meters long. How many centimeters of wrapping paper does he have?

10. The Kwan family traveled 35,000 meters to get to the nearest amusement park. How many kilometers did they have to travel?

☐ **I can convert measurement units within a measurement system.**

The word **mass** is similar to the word **weight**.

1 gram (g) is about the mass of a dollar bill.

1 kilogram (kg) is used to measure the mass of larger objects. A newborn baby would usually weigh 3 to 4 kilograms.

1,000 grams (g) = 1 kilogram (kg)

Circle the most reasonable unit of measurement.

1. a sack of potatoes   5 kg   5 g   2. a quarter   6 g   6 kg

3. a cat $3\frac{1}{2}$ g $3\frac{1}{2}$ kg   4. a fifth grader   34 g   34 kg

Write the equivalent weight.

5. 7 kg = _____ g   6. 6,000 g = _____ kg

7. 12 kg = _____ g   8. 73,000 g = _____ kg

9. An extra-large pizza weighs 2 kilograms. How many grams does it weigh?

10. If the pizza in the above problem is divided equally into 8 slices, how many grams does each slice weigh?

11. If a child's stomach can hold 750 grams of pizza, how many slices of pizza can it hold?

☐ **I can convert measurement units within a measurement system.**

Name_____

Place the liquid measurements in the beakers on the line plot. Use the line plot to answer the questions.

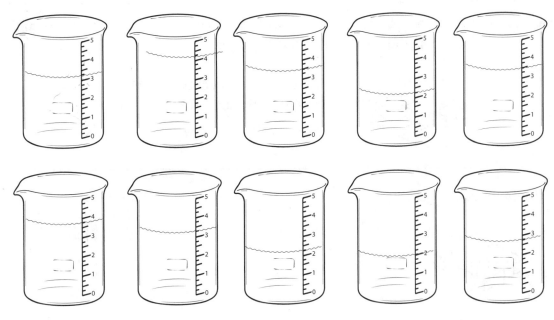

1. ├───┤

2. How many beakers hold at least $2\frac{1}{2}$ ounces? What fraction of the set is that?	3. How much liquid does the set contain in all?
4. This set of beakers is a sample of a larger set. If the original set was 5 times larger, how much liquid did the original set contain?	5. If the liquid in this set was redistributed equally, how much liquid would each beaker contain?

☐ **I can make a line plot displaying fractions and solve problems using the line plot.**

Find the volume of each figure.

Volume tells the number of cubic units within a solid figure. Each cube represents one cubic unit. To find volume, count the number of cubes within the figure.

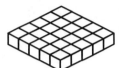

There are 25 total cubes, so the volume is 25 cubic units.

Volume (V) = 25 cubic units

Find the volume of each figure.

1.

V = _____ cubic units

2.

V = _____ cubic units

3.

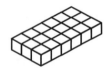

V = _____ cubic units

4.

V = _____ cubic units

5.

V = _____ cubic units

6.

V = _____ cubic units

☐ I understand the concept of volume and can recognize one cubic unit of volume.
☐ I understand that volume is measured using cubic units to completely fill a solid figure.
☐ I can measure volumes using various units.

Find the volume of each figure.

1.

V = _____ cubic units

2.

V = _____ cubic units

3.

V = _____ cubic units

4.

V = _____ cubic units

5.

V = _____ cubic units

6.

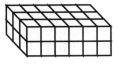

V = _____ cubic units

☐ I can recognize one cubic unit of volume.
☐ I understand that volume is measured using cubic units to completely fill a solid figure.
☐ I can measure volumes using various units.

Name_____

Volume tells the number of cubic units within a solid figure. To find the volume of a rectangular prism, multiply the length by the width by the height ($V = l \times w \times h$).

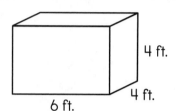

Volume (V) = length × width × height

V = 6 ft. × 4 ft. × 4 ft.

V = 96 ft.³

Find the volume of each figure.

1.

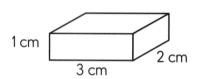

V = _____ cm³

2.

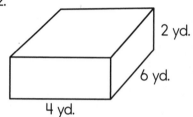

V = _____ yd.³

3.

V = _____ m³

4.

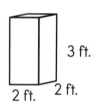

V = _____ ft.³

5.

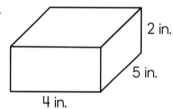

V = _____ in.³

6.

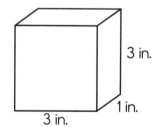

V = _____ in.³

7.

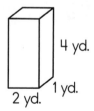

V = _____ yd.³

8.

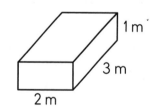

V = _____ m³

9.

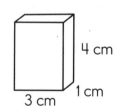

V = _____ cm³

☐ **I can find the volume of a right rectangular prism by using models and formulas.**

Volume tells the number of cubic units within a solid figure. To find the volume of a rectangular prism, multiply the length by the width by the height ($V = l \times w \times h$).

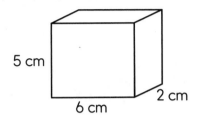

5 cm

6 cm

2 cm

Volume (V) = $l \times w \times h$
V = 6 cm × 2 cm × 5 cm
V = 60 cm³

Find the volume of each figure. Label your answer.

1.

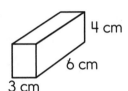

4 cm

6 cm

3 cm

V =_____

2.

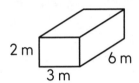

2 m

6 m

3 m

V =_____

3.

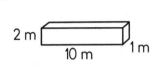

2 m

10 m

1 m

V =_____

4.

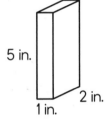

5 in.

2 in.

1 in.

V =_____

5.

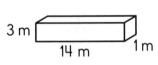

3 m

14 m

1 m

V =_____

6.

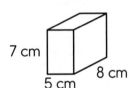

7 cm

5 cm

8 cm

V =_____

7.

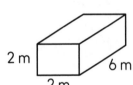

2 m

2 m

6 m

V =_____

8.

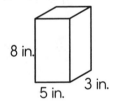

8 in.

5 in.

3 in.

V =_____

Use the given dimensions to find the volume of each rectangular prism. Label your answer.

9. l = 2 cm
    w = 4 cm
    h = 3 cm

10. l = 5 m
    w = 3 m
    h = 4 m

11. l = 10 in.
    w = 3 in.
    h = 5 in.

12. l = 3.5 ft.
    w = 1 ft.
    h = 2 ft.

V =_____   V =_____   V =_____   V =_____

☐ **I can find the volume of a right rectangular prism by using models and formulas.**

5.MD.5, 5.MD.5a, 5.MD.5b

For each problem, sketch a picture of the figure. Then, find the volume.

1. rectangular fish aquarium with height 15 inches, length 20 inches, and width 10 inches

2. shoe box with length 12 inches, height 6 inches, and width 6 inches

3. rectangular cooler with length 24 inches, height 18 inches, and width 12 inches

4. filing cabinet with height 48 inches, width 18 inches, and length 30 inches

☐ I can find the volume of a right rectangular prism by using models and formulas.

Volume = *l* × *w* × *h*

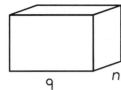

5 × 9 × *n* = 90

45 × *n* = 90

What, when multiplied by 45, equals 90?

n = 2

Complete the table with the missing measurements.

	Length	Width	Height	Volume
1.	4 inches	12 inches		48 cubic inches
2.	6 feet		3 feet	36 cubic feet
3.		9 centimeters	2 centimeters	54 cubic centimeters
4.	2 meters	2 meters	2 meters	
5.	4 inches		3 inches	84 cubic inches
6.	3 yards	6 yards		36 cubic yards
7.	9 inches	7 inches	7 inches	
8.		13 centimeters	4 centimeters	416 cubic centimeters
9.	3 feet		8 feet	192 cubic feet
10.	6 millimeters	5 millimeters	9 millimeters	

☐ **I can use formulas to find the volume of rectangular prisms.**

Name_____

You can use *l* × *w* to find the area of a rectangle. This is also called the **base**.

3 × 4 = 12 square units

Then, multiply the *base* times the *height*, or *b* × *h*, to find the volume.

12 × 4 = 48 cubic units

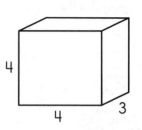

For each problem, sketch a picture of the figure. Then, find the volume.

1. base area = 6 square inches
    height = 3 inches

    V = _____

2. base area = 9 square centimeters
    height = 10 centimeters

    V = _____

3. base area = 42 square feet
    height = 7 feet

    V = _____

4. base area = 20 square inches
    height = 6 inches

    V = _____

5. base area = 55 square centimeters
    height = 6 centimeters

    V = _____

6. base area = 112 square yards
    height = 8 yards

    V = _____

☐ I understand that the volume of a right prism can be found by multiplying the area of
the base by the height.
☐ I can use formulas to find the volume of rectangular prisms.

Name_____

For each problem, sketch a picture of the figure. Then, find the volume.

1. An aquarium is shaped like a rectangular prism and is 20 inches wide, 15 inches tall, and 15 inches long. How many cubic inches of water can the aquarium hold?

2. A moving box is 1 meter wide, $\frac{1}{2}$ meter long, and $\frac{3}{4}$ meter tall. How many cubic meters can the box hold?

3. A rectangular bathtub has dimensions of 2 feet deep by 2 feet wide by 5 feet long. If you only fill the bathtub to a depth of 18 inches, how many cubic inches of water is in the tub?

☐ I can convert units within a measurement system.
☐ I can apply volume formulas to solve real-world problems.

You can find the volume of more complex figures using addition.

First, split the shape into two rectangular prisms.

Then, find the volume of each prism.

2 cm × 2 cm × 7 cm = 28 cubic cm

4 cm × 7 cm × 7 cm = 196 cubic cm

Finally, add the two volumes together.

28 cubic cm + 196 cubic cm = 224 cubic cm

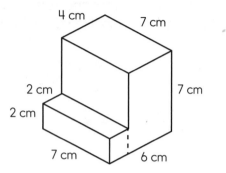

Find the volume of each figure.

1.

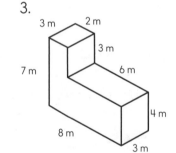

2.

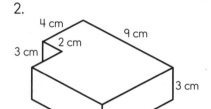

3.

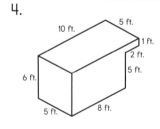

4.

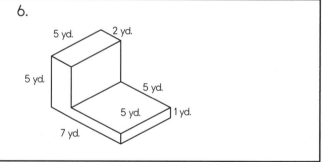

5.

6.

I understand that volume can be added.
I can find the volume of complex rectangular prisms.

A **grid** can be used to show an object's location. It has numbered or lettered lines.

Example: To find the location of the 🌷, move along the bottom horizontal line and find the lettered line the flower is on. Then, move up the line vertically and trace across to see what numbered line it is on. This flower is located at (F, 3).

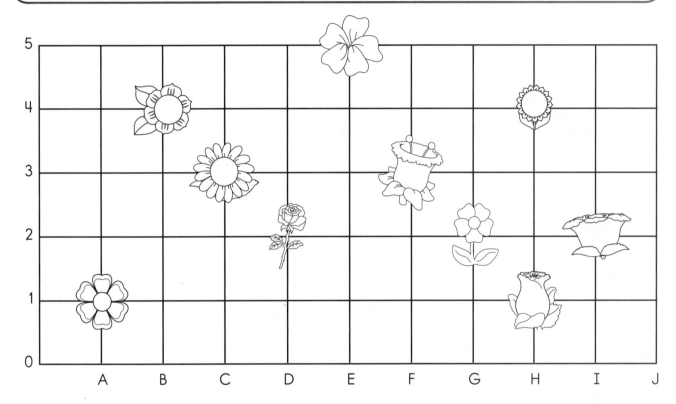

Use the grid above to write the location of each plant.

1. 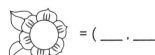 = (___ , ___)   2. 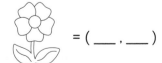 = (___ , ___)   3. 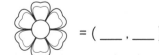 = (___ , ___)

4. = (___ , ___)   5. = (___ , ___)   6. = (___ , ___)

7. = (___ , ___)   8. = (___ , ___)   9. = (___ , ___)

☐ I understand a coordinate system and coordinates.

An **ordered pair** can be used to locate a point on a grid or coordinate graph. An ordered pair looks like this: (2,3). The first number tells how many units the point is located to the right of zero. The second number tells how many units the point is located up from zero.

Example: Find (2,3). Move right 2, and up 3.

Write the letters in order on the lines provided for each ordered pair.

1. (4,6) _____   2. (7,7) _____   3. (5,1) _____   4. (1,1) _____

5. (1,1) _____   6. (1,4) _____   7. (6,2) _____   8. (4,3) _____

9. (0,5) _____   10. (8,3) _____   11. (2,7) _____   12. (6,5) _____

13. (3,2) _____   14. (1,4) _____   15. (5,1) _____   16. (5,1) _____

17. (1,1) _____   18. (1,4) _____   19. (4,3) _____   20. (2,7) _____

21. (2,4) _____   22. (8,1) _____   23. (5,1) _____   24. (7,4) _____

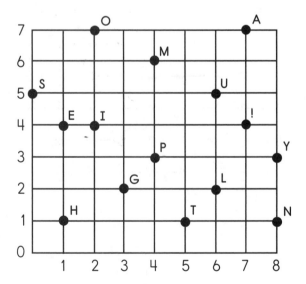

What is the secret message?

_____

_____

I understand a coordinate system and coordinates.

An **ordered pair** can be used to locate a point on a grid or coordinate graph. An ordered pair looks like this: (2,4). The first number tells how many units the point is located to the right of zero. The second number tells how many units the point is located up from zero.

Example: Find (2,4). Move right 2, and up 4.

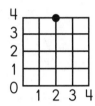

Write the letters for each ordered pair to find the message.

___ ___ ___ ___   ___ ___   ___ ___ ___   ___ ___   ___ ___ ___
(2,1) (4,5) (1,3) (8,3)   (1,0) (4,1)   (5,4) (7,1) (1,5)   (5,4) (4,3)   (1,3) (8,3) (1,5)

___ ___ ___ ___ ___ ___ ___ ___ ___ ___   ___ ___ ___
(1,0) (7,1) (7,4) (5,1) (1,5) (6,6) (1,0) (1,5) (7,1) (1,3) (4,1)   (4,3) (5,4) (5,1)

___ ___ ___ ___ ___ ___
(2,1) (4,5) (6,3) (1,0) (7,1) (7,4)

___ ___ ___ ___   ___ ___ ___ ___.
(1,2) (1,0) (4,3) (1,5)   (4,3) (3,3) (7,1) (6,2)

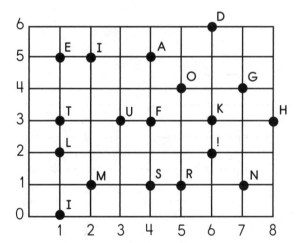

A **polygon** is a closed plane figure formed by three or more line segments with two sides meeting at each vertex.

triangle

quadrilateral

square

rectangle

rhombus

parallelogram

pentagon

hexagon

octagon

trapezoid

Identify each figure. Then, circle all of the quadrilaterals.

1.

_____

2.

_____

3.

_____

4.
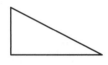
_____

5.

_____

6.

_____

7.
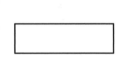
_____

8.

_____

9.

_____

10.

_____

11.

_____

12.

_____

13.

_____

14.

_____

15.

_____

16.

_____

☐ I understand that two-dimensional figures within a category share the same attributes.
☐ I can classify two-dimensional figures into categories.

A **quadrilateral** has 4 sides.

A **trapezoid** is a quadrilateral that has exactly 1 pair of parallel sides.

A **parallelogram** is a quadrilateral that has 2 pairs of parallel sides.

A **rectangle** is a parallelogram that has 4 right angles.

A **square** is a rectangle that has four equal sides.

Classify the following quadrilaterals. Some shapes may have more than one correct classification.

(A) quadrilateral   (B) trapezoid   (C) parallelogram   (D) rectangle   (E) square

1.

 _____

2.

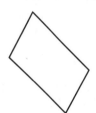 _____

3.

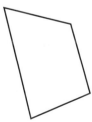 _____

4.

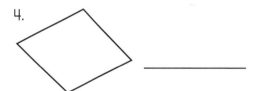 _____

5.

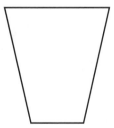 _____

6.

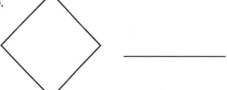 _____

☐ I understand that two-dimensional figures within a category share the same attributes.
☐ I can classify two-dimensional figures into categories.

Name the quadrilateral(s) described.

1. I have 4 sides and 4 right angles.

2. I have 4 sides, and opposite sides are parallel.

3. I have 4 sides and only 1 pair of parallel sides.

4. I have 4 congruent sides, and opposite sides are parallel.

5. I have 4 sides, 2 obtuse angles, and 2 acute angles.

6. I have 4 congruent sides, and opposite angles are equal.

☐ I understand that two-dimensional figures within a category share the same attributes.
☐ I can classify two-dimensional figures by their attributes.

Answer Key

Page 12
1. 4; 2. 6; 3. 24; 4. 90; 5. 100; 6. 200

Page 13
1. 10; 2. 45; 3. 36; 4. 15; 5. 96; 6. 16; 7. 5; 8. 19

Page 14
1. (5 + 6) × 3; 2. (15 – 7) × 4; 3. 2 × [20 – (6 + 10)];
4. (5 + 6) × (3 + 4); 5. (4 + 6) × 7; 6. (5 + 9) ÷ 2

Page 15
1. Subtract 1 from 3 and then add 5. 2. Add 3 and 6, subtract 1 from 2, and then multiply the answers. 3. Add 6 and 12 and then divide your answer by 3. 4. Add 4 and 2, subtract the sum from 10, and then add 4 to your answer. 5. Add 12 and 6, add 3 and 3, and then divide the first answer by the second answer.

Page 16
1. Subtract 7 and 1, then multiply the answer by 4. 2. Add 3 and 7, add 2 and 1, then subtract the answers. 3. Add 3 and 6 and subtract the answer from 47; 4. Multiply 25 and 2, then divide 50 by your answer. 5. Subtract 5 and 3, multiply the answer by 8, then subtract the answer from 21. 6. Add 5 and 1, multiply the answer by 5, then divide that answer by 2. 7. Subtract 3 from 19, then divide by 8. 8. Add 2 and 1, then multiply by 4. Divide 22 by 11, then add 18. Then, multiply both answers.

Page 17
1. H; 2. A; 3. G; 4. B; 5. F; 6. C; 7. E; 8. D

Page 18
1. albums increase by 1, records increase by 2 million; 2. 1, 3, 5, 7, 9; 3. (2,3), (3,5), (4,7), (5,9); 4. Check students' graphs. 5. 9

Page 19
1. laps increase by 2, breaths increase by 1; 2. 2, 3, 4, 5, 6; 3. (2,2), (4,3), (6,4), (8,5), (10,6); 4. Check students' graphs. 5. 6

Page 20
1. 8.5; 2. 50; 3. 23.5; 4. 50; 5. 15.3; 6. 512.5; 7. 150.5; 8. Answers will vary.

Page 21
1. two places right; 2. five places right; 3. three places left; 4. one place left; 5. two places left; 6. two places right; 7. four places right; 8. four places left

Page 22
1. 0.6, 6, 60, 6; 2. 43, 430, 4,300, 43; 3. 653, 10.9, 213, 0.07; 4. 46, 460, 46, 4.6; 5. 3,900, 0.045, 3, 12,600; 6. 123.4, 110, 1,100, 11,000

Page 23
1. <; 2. <; 3. <; 4. >; 5. >; 6. >; 7. >; 8. >; 9. <; 10. <; 11. <; 12. =; 13. <; 14. >; 15. =; 16. <; 17. <; 18. >

Page 24
1. $\frac{3}{10}$; 2. one and twelve hundredths, $1\frac{12}{100}$;
3. 0.221, $\frac{221}{1000}$; 4. 0.53, fifty-three hundredths;
5. eight hundred seventy-one thousandths, $\frac{871}{1000}$;
6. 2.01, two and one hundredth

Page 25
1. $\frac{2}{10}$, 0.2; 2. $\frac{8}{10}$, 0.8; 3. $\frac{9}{10}$, 0.9; 4. $\frac{1}{10}$, 0.1; 5. $\frac{13}{100}$, 0.13;
6. $\frac{87}{100}$, 0.87; 7. $\frac{55}{100}$, 0.55

Page 26
1. 4.55; 2. 10.75; 3. 2.52; 4. 1.847; 5. 89.90

Page 27
1. 0.6; 2. 1.0; 3. 1.6; 4. 3.1; 5. 6.35; 6. 3.15; 7. 0.01; 8. 2.59; 9. 3.0, 3.02; 10. 30.0, 29.96

Page 28
1. 290,322; 2. 372,723; 3. 572,286; 4. 856,304; 5. 260,766; 6. 82,369; 7. 332,762; 8. 136,125; 9. 236,572; 10. 171,720; 11. 39,449; 12. 157,320; 13. 380,328; 14. 315,864; 15. 750,339; 16. 1,101,790; 17. 1,210,808; 18. 480,075; 19. 385,985; 20. 547,328; 21. 544,887; 22. 1,194,132; 23. 1,028,526; 24. 281,352; 25. 795,918

Answer Key

Page 29

1. 18r29; 2. 22r19; 3. 260r9; 4. 31r23; 5. 222r8; 6. 252r3; 7. 42r3; 8. 122r61; 9. 96r7; 10. 50r47; 11. 2,333r1; 12. 2,025r43

Page 30

S 1,944; O 104r2; E 57,762; Y 4r1; K 1,484; A 61r4; D 28,288; W 6r52; J 138,788; U 453r2; F 5,844; L 10,080; T 98r42; N 61,318; C 237r11; R 209,746; I 106r29; H 236r13; just fine, tanks; worse dish year; classy

Page 31

1. $23.74; 2. $40.79; 3. $74.71; 4A. $46.05; B. 42.5 mph; 5. $75

Page 32

1. 6.81 minutes, yes; 2. 11.54 seconds; 3. 11.77 seconds; 4. weeks 1 and 4; 5. 42.19 miles; 6. 63.89 miles; 7. 3.1 meters; 8. 3.7 meters

Page 33

1. 1,596.8, 159.68, 15.968, 159.68, 1.5968; 2. 1,802.4, 180.24, 18.024, 180.24, 1.8024; 3. 1,251.0, 125.10, 12.510, 125.10, 1.2510; 4. 7.92, 25.56, 13.09, 8.76, 69.84; 5. 91.14, 138.82, 172.02, 21.142, 9.971; 6. 65.1472, 40.6244, 31.2806, 86.8042, 3.6834

Page 34

1. $1.88 \times 1.2 = 2.256$; 2. $5.19 \times 0.32 = 1.6608$; 3. $8.76 \times 4.3 = 37.668$; 4. $25.6 \times 3.1 = 79.36$; 5. $4.32 \times 2.1 = 9.072$; 6. $14.9 \times 2.7 = 40.23$; 7. $1.51 \times 4.5 = 6.795$; 8. $3.12 \times 0.61 = 1.9032$

Page 35

1. 63.65; 2. 56.08; 3. 136.8; 4. 0.63; 5. 116.56; 6. 21

Page 36

1. 22.5; 2. 20; 3. 4.13; 4. 5.60; 5. 42.55; 6. 2.31; 7. 36.5; 8. 23.8

Page 37

1. 0.3; 2. 0.03; 3. 0.23; 4. 0.023; 5. 22.7; 6. 2.27; 7. $4.91; 8. 0.03; 9. 20.1; 10. 2.01; 11. 0.61; 12. $0.46; 13. 0.98; 14. 1.84; 15. 0.94; 16. $1.30; 17. 0.105; 18. 8.353; 19. $108.64; 20. 0.04

Page 38

1. 0.54; 2. 1.15; 3. 0.95; 4. 1.825; 5. 0.3125; 6. 0.0775; 7. 1.62; 8. 1.575; 9. 0.146; 10. 1.05; 11. 0.838; 12. 0.748; 13. 13.35; 14. 0.065; 15. 15.004; 16. 0.535; 17. 1.34; 18. 0.325; 19. 0.2125; 20. 0.175

Page 39

1. 9; 2. 0.2; 3. 9.9; 4. 0.85; 5. 6.2; 6. 7; 7. 5; 8. 38; 9. 3; 10. 4.3; 11. 15; 12. 0.3125; 13. 2.125; 14. 33.875; 15. 2.7; 16. 0.25

Page 40

1. 200 trombones; 2. 0.055 watts; 3. about 28 pianos; 4A. 19.14 watts; B. 6.38 watts; 5. 11 pianos; 6. 0.08 watts; 7. 24 watts

Page 41

1. $0.66; 2. $0.42; 3. $0.22; 4. $0.04; 5. $0.19; 6. $0.02

Page 42

1. 6, $\frac{4}{6}$, $\frac{5}{6}$; 2. 4, $\frac{2}{4}$, $\frac{1}{4}$; 3. 10, $\frac{4}{10}$, $\frac{1}{10}$; 4. 12, $\frac{9}{12}$, $\frac{1}{12}$; 5. 14, $\frac{2}{14}$, $\frac{2}{14}$; 6. 9, $\frac{6}{9}$, $\frac{3}{9}$; 7. 10, $\frac{1}{10}$, $\frac{6}{10}$; 8. 6, $\frac{3}{8}$, $\frac{4}{8}$; 9. 20, $\frac{6}{8}$, $\frac{5}{8}$

Page 43

1. $1\frac{1}{9}$; 2. $\frac{7}{8}$; 3. $\frac{7}{10}$; 4. $1\frac{1}{8}$; 5. $1\frac{1}{6}$; 6. $\frac{7}{15}$; 7. $\frac{5}{6}$; 8. $1\frac{5}{8}$; 9. $1\frac{3}{8}$; 10. $\frac{7}{8}$; 11. $\frac{13}{14}$; 12. $1\frac{1}{4}$

Page 44

1. $5\frac{13}{24}$; 2. $5\frac{19}{20}$; 3. $7\frac{1}{6}$; 4. $5\frac{11}{12}$; 5. $7\frac{1}{4}$; 6. $7\frac{11}{15}$; 7. $6\frac{11}{12}$; 8. $4\frac{1}{24}$; 9. $7\frac{1}{4}$; 10. $5\frac{1}{10}$; 11. $9\frac{7}{8}$; 12. $12\frac{3}{22}$

Page 45

1. $\frac{5}{12}$; 2. $\frac{3}{10}$; 3. $\frac{1}{6}$; 4. $\frac{3}{14}$; 5. $\frac{5}{18}$; 6. $\frac{8}{21}$; 7. $\frac{11}{20}$; 8. $\frac{18}{35}$; 9. $\frac{17}{45}$; 10. $\frac{19}{40}$; 11. $\frac{29}{42}$; 12. $\frac{43}{66}$

Page 46

1. $4\frac{1}{8}$; 2. $2\frac{2}{3}$; 3. $5\frac{2}{9}$; 4. $3\frac{3}{5}$; 5. $7\frac{1}{5}$; 6. $4\frac{5}{9}$; 7. $11\frac{8}{11}$; 8. $8\frac{1}{9}$; 9. $6\frac{2}{3}$; 10. $9\frac{4}{5}$; 11. $11\frac{3}{10}$; 12. $7\frac{1}{6}$

Answer Key

Page 47

1. $1\frac{5}{6}$; 2. $\frac{23}{24}$; 3. $1\frac{3}{4}$; 4. $3\frac{4}{15}$; 5. $\frac{5}{8}$; 6. $\frac{5}{9}$; 7. $1\frac{5}{6}$; 8. $1\frac{7}{10}$;
9. $1\frac{17}{24}$; 10. $3\frac{3}{8}$; 11. $3\frac{1}{2}$; 12. $\frac{3}{4}$

Page 48

1.

$1\frac{4}{5}$	($\frac{1}{10}$)	$2\frac{3}{5}$
($2\frac{3}{10}$)	$1\frac{1}{2}$	($\frac{7}{10}$)
($\frac{2}{5}$)	$2\frac{9}{10}$	$1\frac{1}{5}$

2.

$\frac{4}{15}$	($\frac{1}{5}$)	$\frac{8}{15}$
($\frac{3}{5}$)	$\frac{1}{3}$	($\frac{1}{15}$)
$\frac{2}{15}$	($\frac{7}{15}$)	$\frac{2}{5}$

3.

$1\frac{1}{8}$	($1\frac{7}{16}$)	$1\frac{3}{8}$
($1\frac{9}{16}$)	($1\frac{5}{16}$)	($1\frac{1}{16}$)
$1\frac{1}{4}$	($1\frac{3}{16}$)	$1\frac{1}{2}$

4.

$2\frac{1}{3}$	($2\frac{1}{18}$)	$2\frac{4}{9}$
($2\frac{7}{18}$)	($2\frac{5}{18}$)	($2\frac{1}{6}$)
$2\frac{1}{9}$	($2\frac{1}{2}$)	$2\frac{2}{9}$

Page 49

1. $1\frac{1}{4}$ cups; 2. 4 cups; 3. $\frac{3}{8}$ cup; 4. $4\frac{1}{8}$ cups;
5. $5\frac{15}{16}$ miles; 6. $3\frac{3}{5}$ miles

Page 50

1A. $3\frac{1}{3}$ more innings; B. $2\frac{1}{3}$ innings; 2. $2\frac{1}{2}$ games;
3. $\frac{5}{8}$ inches; 4. $\frac{7}{24}$ more fans; 5. $\frac{19}{24}$ of his money;
6. 6:45 pm

Page 51

1. $\frac{5}{12}$; 2A. $\frac{11}{12}$; B. $\frac{1}{12}$; 3A. $\frac{3}{4}$; B. $\frac{1}{4}$; 4. $6\frac{1}{3}$ minutes

Page 52

1. $3\frac{11}{12}$ hours; 2. $\frac{7}{12}$ hours; 3. $\frac{2}{3}$ hours; 4. $2\frac{5}{12}$ hours;
5. $1\frac{1}{12}$ hours; 6. Tyrone

Page 53

1. $7\frac{1}{2}$; 2. $1\frac{3}{4}$; 3. $2\frac{6}{7}$; 4. $8\frac{3}{5}$; 5. $2\frac{7}{8}$; 6. $4\frac{1}{5}$; 7. $2\frac{7}{12}$; 8. $2\frac{1}{2}$;
9. $1\frac{5}{8}$; 10. $2\frac{3}{4}$; 11. $5\frac{4}{9}$; 12. $6\frac{5}{6}$; 13. $7\frac{2}{3}$; 14. $11\frac{1}{4}$; 15. 12;
16. $3\frac{2}{7}$; 17. 12; 18. 8

Page 54

1. $\frac{1}{4}$ pie; 2. $\frac{2}{3}$ cup; 3. $1\frac{1}{2}$ cups; 4. $\frac{1}{2}$ foot;
5. $6\frac{1}{4}$ pounds; 6. $1\frac{1}{3}$ cups

Page 55

1. $\frac{2}{15}$; 2. $\frac{1}{12}$; 3. $\frac{1}{4}$; 4. $\frac{3}{8}$; 5. $\frac{3}{10}$; 6. $\frac{1}{6}$

Page 56

1. $\frac{3}{8}$; 2. $\frac{2}{15}$; 3. $\frac{2}{15}$; 4. $\frac{5}{12}$; 5. $\frac{3}{32}$; 6. $\frac{5}{24}$; 7. $\frac{5}{14}$; 8. $\frac{1}{12}$;
9. $\frac{2}{25}$; 10. $\frac{3}{10}$; 11. $\frac{9}{20}$; 12. $\frac{3}{32}$; 13. $\frac{6}{25}$; 14. $\frac{1}{4}$; 15. $\frac{4}{0}$;
16. $\frac{3}{16}$; 17. $\frac{5}{21}$; 18. $\frac{3}{14}$; 19. $\frac{5}{24}$; 20. $\frac{5}{18}$; 21. $\frac{3}{35}$; 22. $\frac{1}{16}$;
23. $\frac{3}{28}$; 24. $\frac{5}{18}$

Page 57

1. 10; 2. $3\frac{1}{4}$; 3. $4\frac{19}{20}$; 4. $2\frac{3}{5}$; 5. $2\frac{6}{25}$; 6. $8\frac{1}{3}$; 7. $7\frac{1}{2}$;
8. $14\frac{7}{10}$; 9. $5\frac{13}{24}$; 10. $2\frac{1}{4}$; 11. $1\frac{27}{28}$; 12. $5\frac{1}{2}$; 13. $6\frac{3}{10}$; 14. $9\frac{1}{3}$;
15. $6\frac{3}{4}$; 16. $7\frac{45}{56}$

Page 58

1. less than, Answers will vary. 2. greater than, Answers will vary. 3. less than, Answers will vary.
4. greater than, Answers will vary. 5. $\frac{1}{3}$; 6. $\frac{13}{2}$;
7. multiply by $\frac{1}{4}$; 32 in. by 40 in.

Answer Key

Page 59

1. $1\frac{1}{6}$ cups; 2. $5\frac{1}{4}$ cups chili powder, $2\frac{1}{4}$ cups olive oil; 3. 2 ounces, 2; 4. $1\frac{1}{3}$; 5. $1\frac{7}{9}$ cups; 6. 2 cups; 7. 401°

Page 60

1. $2\frac{2}{5}$ miles; 2. $\frac{3}{5}$ gallon; 3. $4.00; 4. $\frac{1}{4}$ barrel; 5. $\frac{3}{5}$ mile

Page 61

1. 3 students; 2. 9 girls; 3. 4 students; 4. $\frac{3}{4}$ hour, or 45 minutes; 5. $1\frac{1}{6}$ hours, or 1 hour 10 minutes

Page 62

1. $\frac{4}{9}$; 2. $\frac{1}{4}$ 3. $5\frac{3}{25}$

Page 63

1. $13\frac{1}{2}$; 2. 35; 3. $\frac{1}{14}$; 4. $\frac{3}{5}$; 5. $\frac{3}{20}$; 6. $\frac{1}{8}$; 7. $\frac{9}{40}$; 8. $\frac{1}{18}$; 9. $\frac{3}{8}$; 10. $\frac{5}{12}$; 11. $\frac{4}{15}$; 12. $\frac{8}{25}$; 13. $\frac{5}{18}$; 14. $\frac{7}{12}$; 15. 12; 16. $12\frac{1}{2}$

Page 64

1. C, 8 pieces; 2. A, $\frac{1}{2}$ cup; 3. E, 8 glasses; 4. B, 2 pots; 5. D, $\frac{1}{8}$ pie; 6. F, $\frac{1}{8}$ teaspoon

Page 65

1. 8; 2. $6\frac{1}{2}$; 3. $1\frac{3}{4}$; 4. $\frac{3}{20}$; 5. $\frac{11}{12}$, 11; 6. $2\frac{1}{3}$; 7. $4\frac{8}{9}$

Page 66

1. 36 sandwiches; 2. 4 batches; 3. $\frac{3}{8}$ cup; 4-5. Answers will vary.

Page 67

1. $1\frac{5}{12}$ cups; 2. $3\frac{3}{4}$ cups; 3. $\frac{1}{6}$ miles; 4. 4 runners; 5. $\frac{1}{4}$ pizza

Page 68

1. $\frac{1}{4}$; 2. $1\frac{1}{4}$ minutes; 3. $15\frac{3}{4}$ feet; 4. $\frac{7}{12}$ hour, or 35 minutes; 5. 56 students

Page 69

1. 1 ft. 2. 38 in. 3. 1 ft. 7 in. 4. 56 in. 5. 2 ft. 6. 7 ft. 7. 6 yd. 8. 26 in. 9. 5 ft. 10. 110 inches; 11. 1 mi. 12. 11,000 ft. 13. 3 mi. 14. 4 mi. 15. 2 mi. 16. 72; 17. 2; 18. 3,520; 19. 2; 20. 6; 21. 18; 22. $\frac{1}{3}$; 23. 10,560; 24. 15; 25. 47; 26. 12; 27. 2; 28. 5; 29. 3; 30. 360; 31. 17,600; 32. 3; 33. 5,280

Page 70

1. fluid ounces, quarts, fluid ounces; 2. gallons, cups; 3. 2; 4. 4; 5. 1; 6. 1; 7. 12; 8. 16; 9. 8; 10. 4; 11. 2; 12. 6; 13. $\frac{1}{2}$; 14. 128; 15. 32; 16. 3; 17. 11; 18. >; 19. <; 20. <; 21. =; 22. >; 23. <; 24. =; 25. >; 26. <

Page 71

1. 6; 2. 48; 3. 14,000; 4. 32,000; 5. 10; 6. 5; 7. 261; 8. 147; 9. 5,000; 10. <; 11. <; 12. <; 13. =; 14. >; 15. <; 16. >; 17. >; 18. <; 19. =; 20. =; 21. =; 22. 25 feet; 23. 7 quarts; 24. 50 pounds

Page 72

1. 3 quarts; 2. 10 ounces; 3. 2 cups; 4. 5,530 feet; 5. 300 feet; 6A. 8 quarts; B. Kade; C. 2 quarts; 7A. 24 inches; B. 4 inches; 8. 12 people

Page 73

1. 4,200; 2. 62; 3. 4,000; 4. 8; 5. 850; 6. 540; 7. greater than; 8. yes; 9. 500 cm; 10. 35 km

Page 74

1. 5 kg; 2. 6 g; 3. $3\frac{1}{2}$ kg; 4. 34 kg; 5. 7,000; 6. 6; 7. 12,000; 8. 73; 9. 2,000 grams; 10. 250 grams; 11. 3 slices

94

Answer Key

Page 75

1.
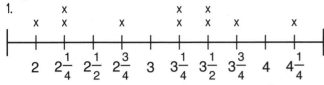

2. 7, $\frac{7}{10}$; 3. $30\frac{3}{4}$ ounces; 4. $153\frac{3}{4}$ ounces; 5. $3\frac{3}{40}$ ounces

Page 76

1. 20; 2. 12; 3. 18; 4. 18; 5. 27; 6. 20

Page 77

1. 13; 2. 14; 3. 20; 4. 10; 5. 40; 6. 36

Page 78

1. 6; 2. 48; 3. 4; 4. 12; 5. 40; 6. 9; 7. 8; 8. 6; 9. 12

Page 79

1. 72 cubic centimeters; 2. 36 cubic meters;
3. 20 cubic meters; 4. 10 cubic inches; 5. 42 cubic
meters; 6. 280 cubic centimeters; 7. 24 cubic
meters; 8. 120 cubic inches; 9. 24 cubic centimeters;
10. 60 cubic meters; 11. 150 cubic inches;
12. 7 cubic feet

Page 80

1. 3,000 cubic inches; 2. 432 cubic inches;
3. 5,184 cubic inches; 4. 25,920 cubic inches

Page 81

1. 1 in. 2. 2 ft. 3. 3 cm; 4. 8 cubic meters; 5. 7 inches;
6. 3 yards; 7. 441 cubic inches; 8. 8 centimeters;
9. 8 feet; 10. 270 cubic millimeters

Page 82

1. 18 cubic inches; 2. 90 cubic cm; 3. 294 cubic feet;
4. 120 cubic inches; 5. 330 cubic centimeters;
6. 896 cubic yards

Page 83

1. 4,500 cubic inches; 2. $\frac{3}{8}$ cubic meter;
3. 25,920 cubic inches

Page 84

1. 38 cubic inches; 2. 171 cubic cm; 3. 114 cubic m;
4. 250 cubic feet; 5. 184 cubic inches;
6. 75 cubic yards

Page 85

1. (D,2); 2. (E,5); 3. (H,4); 4. (H,1); 5. (C,3); 6. (I,2);
7. (B,4); 8. (G,2); 9. (A,1)

Page 86

1. M; 2. A; 3. T; 4. H; 5. H; 6. E; 7. L; 8. P; 9. S; 10. Y;
11. O; 12. U; 13. G; 14. E; 15. T; 16. T; 17. H; 18. E; 19. P;
20. O; 21. I; 22. N; 23. T; 24. !; Math helps you get
the point!

Page 87

Math is one of the ingredients for making life fun.

Page 88

1. rhombus; 2. octagon; 3. trapezoid; 4. triangle;
5. square; 6. pentagon; 7. rectangle;
8. parallelogram; 9. hexagon; 10. triangle;
11. quadrilateral; 12. parallelogram; 13. rectangle;
14. pentagon; 15. quadrilateral; 16. square

Page 89

1. A, C, D; 2. A, C; 3. A, B; 4. A, C; 5. A, B; 6. A, C, D, E

Page 90

1. rectangle or square; 2. square, rectangle,
parallelogram, or rhombus; 3. trapezoid; 4. square
or rhombus; 5. parallelogram or rhombus;
6. square, rectangle, parallelogram, or rhombus

Notes

© Carson-Dellosa • CD-104606